GoodFood

101 Italian feasts

10 9 8 7 6 5 4 3 2 1

Published in 2010 by BBC Books, an imprint of Ebury Publishing
A Random House Group company

Photographs © BBC Magazines 2010
Recipes © BBC Magazines 2010
Book design © Woodlands Books Ltd 2010
All recipes contained in this book first appeared in BBC *Good Food* magazine

The Random House Group Limited
Reg. No. 954009

Addresses for companies within the Random House Group can be found at www.randomhouse.co.uk

A CIP catalogue record for this book is available from the British Library

The Random House Group Limited supports The Forest Stewardship Council (FSC), the leading international
forest certification organization. All our titles that are printed on Greenpeace approved FSC certified paper
carry the FSC logo. Our paper procurement policy can be found at www.rbooks.co.uk/environment

To buy books by your favourite authors and register for offers visit www.rbooks.co.uk

Printed and bound by Firmengruppe APPL, aprinta druck, Wemding, Germany
Colour origination by Dot Gradations Ltd, UK

Commissioning Editor: Muna Reyal
Project Editor: Joe Cottington
Designer: Kathryn Gammon
Production: Rebecca Jones
Picture Researcher: Gabby Harrington

ISBN: 9781846079719

Picture credits

BBC *Good Food* magazine and BBC Books would like to thank the following people for providing photos. While every effort
has been made to trace and acknowledge all photographers, we should like to apologise should there be any errors or
omissions.

Iain Bagwell p63; Peter Cassidy p35, p97, p111, p147, p177, p187, p209; Jean Cazals p115, p149, p169; Ken Field p89; Will Heap
p61, p173; Lisa Linder p151; Gareth Morgans p13, p51, p59, p95; David Munns p27, p29, p33, p37, p39, p41, p43, p45, p47,
p65, p67, p73, p75, p79, p85, p107, p119, p131, p135, p137, p139, p143, p145, p167, p203, p205; Noel Murphy p117, p159,
p183; Myles New p11, p19, p21, p31, p57, p81, p83, p87, p93, p103, p105, p109, p113, p127, p129, p133, p179, p181, p185,
p197; Elisabeth Parsons p17, p23, p25, p49, p53, p55, p99, p155, p157, p165, p191, p195, p199, p211; Brett Stevens p171;
Roger Stowell p123; Debi Treloar p163, p121; Simon Walton p69, p91, p141; Cameron Watt p153; Philip Webb p15, p71, p77,
p101, p125, p161, p175, p189, p193, p201; Simon Wheeler p207

All the recipes in this book were created by the editorial team at *Good Food* and by regular contributors to BBC Magazines.

GoodFood
101 Italian feasts

Editor **Jane Hornby**

BBC BOOKS

Contents

Introduction

It's no wonder we've all fallen for Italian cooking; from quick suppers to sublime desserts, Italian food is always seasonal, inspired by ingredients, yet simple at its heart. This little book is full of endlessly versatile recipes from *Good Food* magazine, for Italian inspiration whatever the occasion.

Pasta comes in all shapes and sizes, so we've included all sorts of ways to cook with it, from simple weeknight spaghetti to classic lasagne for a crowd. Our simple suppers, such as a *Simple squash risotto* (pictured left) for example, need either little shopping or little prep – or little of both! The only challenge is choosing what to make.

When cooking for friends or family I'll often turn to Italian – a recipe with big flavours that will please everyone (and which, more often than not, is easy to prep ahead and cook later). So many of the meat dishes, sauces, starters and sides within this book lend themselves to stress-free entertaining. Round off a meal with a silky semifreddo or coffee and homemade biscotti for the full Italian experience. Much classic Italian cooking is meat-free, too, so there's also plenty of choice here for vegetarian cooks.

Many recipes in this book are authentic, some simply an Italian twist on a favourite, but whatever their origin, they've all gone through our test kitchen with flying colours. Choose quality ingredients, cook them simply and cook them with love – and soon you'll be speaking Italian in the kitchen, if nowhere else…

Jane Hornby
Good Food magazine

Notes and conversion tables

NOTES ON THE RECIPES

• Eggs are large in the UK and Australia and extra large in America unless stated otherwise.

• Wash fresh produce before preparation.

• Recipes contain nutritional analyses for 'sugar', which means the total sugar content including all natural sugars in the ingredients, unless otherwise stated.

OVEN TEMPERATURES

Gas	°C	°C Fan	°F	Oven temp.
¼	110	90	225	Very cool
½	120	100	250	Very cool
1	140	120	275	Cool or slow
2	150	130	300	Cool or slow
3	160	140	325	Warm
4	180	160	350	Moderate
5	190	170	375	Moderately hot
6	200	180	400	Fairly hot
7	220	200	425	Hot
8	230	210	450	Very hot
9	240	220	475	Very hot

APPROXIMATE WEIGHT CONVERSIONS

• All the recipes in this book list both imperial and metric measurements. Conversions are approximate and have been rounded up or down. Follow one set of measurements only; do not mix the two.

• Cup measurements, which are used by cooks in Australia and America, have not been listed here as they vary from ingredient to ingredient. Kitchen scales should be used to measure dry/solid ingredients.

Good Food is concerned about sustainable sourcing and animal welfare. Where possible, humanely reared meats, sustainably caught fish (see fishonline.org for further information from the Marine Conservation Society) and free-range chickens and eggs are used when recipes are originally tested.

SPOON MEASURES

Spoon measurements are level unless otherwise specified.

- 1 teaspoon (tsp) = 5ml
- 1 tablespoon (tbsp) = 15ml
- 1 Australian tablespoon = 20ml (cooks in Australia should measure 3 teaspoons where 1 tablespoon is specified in a recipe)

APPROXIMATE LIQUID CONVERSIONS

metric	imperial	AUS	US
50ml	2fl oz	¼ cup	¼ cup
125ml	4fl oz	½ cup	½ cup
175ml	6fl oz	¾ cup	¾ cup
225ml	8fl oz	1 cup	1 cup
300ml	10fl oz/½ pint	½ pint	1¼ cups
450ml	16fl oz	2 cups	2 cups/1 pint
600ml	20fl oz/1 pint	1 pint	2½ cups
1 litre	35fl oz/1¾ pints	1¾ pints	1 quart

Pizza rolls

Kids will love these tasty stuffed rolls. Vary the fillings to whatever they like best on pizza – salami, blue cheese or roasted vegetables also work well.

TAKES 30 MINUTES ● MAKES 6 ROLLS

6 crusty bread rolls
2 tbsp tomato purée
6 slices ham
3 tomatoes, sliced
2 balls mozzarella, sliced
2 tsp dried oregano
6 black olives (optional)
salad, to serve

1 Heat oven to 180C/160C fan/gas 4. Cut the tops off the rolls and scoop out and discard the insides. Spread the rolls with tomato purée, then fill each with a slice of ham, some tomato and finally the mozzarella. Sprinkle over the dried oregano and top each with an olive, if you like.

2 Place the rolls on a baking sheet and bake for 15 minutes until the rolls are crusty brown and the cheese is bubbling. Leave to rest for 1 minute, then serve hot with a side salad.

PER ROLL 275 kcals, protein 17g, carbs 30g, fat 11g, sat fat 6g, fibre 2g, sugar 4g, salt 1.99g

Tuna & caper panzanella

Panzanella salads are traditional in Italy as a way to make the most of old bread. If you don't have ciabatta, use any country loaf with a good crust, or pitta bread.

TAKES 15 MINUTES ● SERVES 2

3 slices ciabatta, preferably a day or
   two old
4–5 tomatoes
½ cucumber
8–10 basil leaves
200g can tuna
2 tsp capers, drained and roughly
   chopped
2 tbsp red wine vinegar
4 tbsp olive oil

1 Dip the bread briefly into cold water then squeeze well and crumble into a bowl. Halve the tomatoes, squeeze the seeds on to the bread, then roughly chop the flesh. Chop the cucumber into small chunks.

2 Add the tomato and cucumber to the bread, then tear in the basil leaves. Drain and flake the tuna into chunks, add to the bread with the capers, vinegar, oil and salt and black pepper to taste. Mix everything together well and serve.

PER SERVING 463 kcals, protein 27g, carbs 21g, fat 31g, sat fat 5g, fibre 3g, sugar 6g, salt 1.35g

Italian mushrooms on toast

Earthy mushrooms are best served simply in a creamy sauce with a hint of garlic. Update a favourite by piling them up on toast and topping with a slice of prosciutto.

TAKES 20 MINUTES ● **SERVES 4**

4 large slices sourdough bread
1 tbsp olive oil
4 slices prosciutto
knob of butter
350g/12oz mixed mushrooms
1 garlic clove, crushed
4 tbsp crème fraîche
handful of flat-leaf parsley leaves, finely chopped

1 Toast the sourdough bread, cut each slice in half then set aside. Heat the oil in a large frying pan and fry the prosciutto for about 2 minutes on each side until golden and crisp. Break the prosciutto into large pieces and set aside on some kitchen paper.

2 Add the butter to the pan followed by the mushrooms. Cook for 2 minutes, then add the garlic and crème fraîche. Cook for 3–5 minutes more until the mushrooms are soft and lightly coated in the crème fraîche. Stir through a little parsley. Pile up on the toasts and top with the prosciutto and the rest of the parsley.

PER SERVING 280 kcals, protein 9g, carbs 28g, fat 16g, sat fat 8g, fibre 3g, sugar 1g, salt 1.37g

Ricotta toasts with rocket & pine nut salsa

Keep things casual and share this starter or light meal from one big plate. The toasts are best made fresh, then loaded up and eaten one at a time to keep them crisp.

TAKES 15 MINUTES • SERVES 2, EASILY DOUBLED

3 anchovy fillets from a can or jar, drained and roughly chopped
½ or 1 garlic clove, roughly chopped, depending on your taste
50g bag wild rocket leaves
20g pack basil, leaves only
1 tbsp capers in brine, drained
zest 1 lemon, juice of 1½
3 tbsp extra virgin olive oil, plus extra to serve
1 tbsp toasted pine nuts
½ 200g tub ricotta
sourdough bread, to serve

1 Put the anchovies, garlic, rocket, basil leaves, capers, lemon zest, juice and olive oil into a food processor and pulse until you have a slightly chunky, bright green sauce. Stir most of the pine nuts through the sauce, spoon into a serving bowl and scatter the remaining pine nuts over the top.

2 Put the ricotta into a mixing bowl, season, then whisk until it becomes creamy and soft. Spoon into a serving bowl, drizzle over a little olive oil and add a grinding of black pepper.

3 When you're ready to eat, heat the grill to high. Cut thin slices of bread, each big enough for a couple of bites. Spread evenly over a baking sheet and grill for 2 minutes on each side until crisp. Drizzle a little oil over each piece of toast, sprinkle with a little flaky sea salt, then serve with the ricotta and salsa.

PER SERVING 279 kcals, protein 8g, carbs 3g, fat 26g, sat fat 6g, fibre 1g, sugar 2g, salt 1.22g

Easy tomato pizzas

Smaller pizzas are easier to handle than big, and the middles cook through more evenly. Believe it or not, these are low in fat!

TAKES 20 MINUTES, PLUS STANDING AND RISING • MAKES 8 SMALL PIZZAS

FOR THE DOUGH

450g/1lb strong white bread flour, plus extra to dust

7g sachet fast-action yeast

2 tbsp extra virgin olive oil, plus extra to grease

FOR THE TOPPING

100g/4oz passata

1 garlic clove, crushed

8 tomatoes (green, orange, red, yellow – all different shapes and sizes), sliced

your choice of toppings: goat's cheese (with rind), grated Parmesan or Parmesan shavings, handfuls of rocket leaves, slices of prosciutto (optional)

1 Mix the flour, yeast and 2 teaspoons salt in a large bowl, and make a well in the middle. Combine the oil with 350ml/12fl oz warm water, then pour the liquid into the bowl. Mix to a sticky dough and set aside for 15 minutes.

2 Turn out the dough on to a well-floured surface then, with floured hands, knead it gently for about 2 minutes. Return the dough to the bowl, cover with oiled cling film and leave in a warm place (or in the fridge overnight) until doubled in size.

3 Heat oven to 240C/220C fan/gas 9. Dust some baking sheets with flour. Split the dough into eight pieces, roll each one into a thin, rough circle, then lift on to the floured sheets. Mix together the passata and garlic, then smear a little over each dough circle. Add some tomato, season, then top with goat's cheese or Parmesan if you like. Bake for 12 minutes, then top with more cheese, rocket or prosciutto.

PER UNTOPPED PIZZA 231 kcals, protein 6g, carbs 45g, fat 5g, sat fat 1g, fibre 3g, sugar 3g, salt 0.53g

Parmesan-baked ricotta with tomato, olive & basil salad

A great idea for a smart light lunch. The ricotta can be baked up to a day ahead and the salad dressing made in advance – just leaving the basil and tomatoes on the day.

TAKES 50 MINUTES ● SERVES 6

3 × 250g tubs ricotta
2 eggs
100g/4oz Parmesan, finely grated
4 large tomatoes
handful of good-quality black olives,
    stones removed
2 tbsp olive oil
1 tbsp extra-virgin olive oil
1 tbsp red wine vinegar
¼ tsp caster sugar
1 garlic clove, crushed
small bunch of basil, leaves only

1 Heat oven to 200C/180C fan/gas 6. Beat together the ricotta and eggs, fold in most of the Parmesan, then season to taste. Line a 900g loaf tin with baking parchment, then scoop the ricotta mixture into the tin. Level the top, scatter with the remaining cheese, then bake for 35 minutes or until set and golden. Leave to cool before turning it out.

2 Slice the tomatoes fairly thickly, then very roughly chop the olives. Whisk together the oils, vinegar, sugar, garlic, olives and seasoning. Just before serving, roughly chop a few of the basil leaves and stir most of them into the dressing.

3 To serve, slice the ricotta and put it on to plates. Toss the tomatoes with most of the dressing. Serve alongside the ricotta, drizzle the rest of the dressing over and scatter with the remaining basil leaves.

PER SERVING 354 kcals, protein 21g, carbs 6g, fat 28g, sat fat 13g, fibre 1g, sugar 6g, salt 0.82g

Artichoke, caper & lemon dip

Better than anything you can buy, this artichoke dip is ideal to serve with drinks.
It's good with warmed pitta bread or breadsticks, or spread over garlicky toasts.

**TAKES 10 MINUTES • SERVES 8 AS
A NIBBLE**

280g jar marinated artichokes, drained
1 garlic clove
50g/2oz pine nuts, toasted, plus extra
   to garnish
zest and juice of 1 lemon
3 tbsp grated Parmesan
20g pack flat-leaf parsley, a few leaves
   reserved
3 tbsp extra-virgin olive oil

1 Combine all the ingredients in a food
processor or blender and season with
salt and black pepper. Whizz to a chunky
purée, then scrape out into a bowl.
2 Sprinkle with extra pine nuts and the
reserved parsley leaves to serve.

PER SERVING 138 kcals, protein 2g, carbs 1g,
fat 14g, sat fat 2g, fibre 1g, sugar 1g, salt 0.47g

Crisp spinach & ricotta tart

Served with a fresh green salad, this crisp tart would make a deliciously light lunch or picnic pie.

TAKES 1 HOUR • SERVES 6

3 eggs, beaten
250g tub ricotta
200g/8oz frozen leaf spinach, defrosted, squeezed dry and chopped
1 spring onion, finely sliced
½ × 145g tub fresh basil pesto
270g pack filo pastry
knob of butter, melted
½ × 240g pack sun-blushed tomatoes in oil, roughly chopped

1 Heat oven to 180C/160C fan/gas 4. Mix together the eggs and ricotta, then add the spinach, spring onion and pesto. Set aside. Unwrap the pastry and cover with a just damp piece of kitchen paper. Mix the butter with 2 tablespoons of the tomato oil.

2 Brush the butter mixture over one sheet of pastry, then put it in a 23cm tart tin. Brush another piece of pastry and put it in the tin, overlapping the first piece a little. Keep brushing and overlapping the pastry sheets (keeping the pastry covered when not using it) until you have used up the pack and the tin is completely covered. Trim away any pastry overhanging the edges of the tin, then bake for 5–10 minutes.

3 Spoon the spinach mixture into the pastry and scatter with the drained tomatoes. Cook for 20–25 minutes until the filling is set. Cool, then cut the tart into slices to serve.

PER SERVING 360 kcals, protein 13g, carbs 31g, fat 21g, sat fat 8g, fibre 1g, sugar 5g, salt 1.78g

Baked figs & goat's cheese with radicchio

There's nothing to this stylish recipe – assemble everything on a baking sheet and it's ready for the oven at a moment's notice.

TAKES ABOUT 30 MINUTES

● **SERVES 6**

oil, for brushing
6 ripe figs
200g/8oz soft goat's cheese
1 radicchio head
85g/3oz walnut pieces

FOR THE DRESSING

6 tbsp olive oil
3 tbsp balsamic vinegar

1 Heat oven to 180C/160C fan/gas 4. Unless the baking sheet is non stick, line it with foil and brush the foil lightly with oil.

2 Cut the figs into quarters, from the top almost to the base, and arrange them on the foil. Slice the goat's cheese and arrange it in the centre of the figs. Bake for 10–15 minutes until the cheese is melted and tinged brown.

3 Meanwhile, whisk the dressing ingredients in a bowl and season.

4 Put a couple of large radicchio leaves on each serving plate, remove the figs from the oven and put them on the radicchio leaves. Scatter the walnuts on top. Drizzle with the dressing and serve warm or at room temperature.

PER SERVING 314 kcals, protein 8g, carbs 7g, fat 28g, sat fat 7g, fibre 2g, added sugar none, salt 0.81g

Warm lentil salad with prosciutto, chicken & rocket

You'll only need the meat from two chicken breasts for this salad, as the lentils and prosciutto are very satisfying.

TAKES 15 MINUTES • SERVES 4

1 red onion, halved and very thinly sliced
1 tbsp sherry vinegar or balsamic vinegar, plus extra to drizzle (optional)
handful of flat-leaf parsley, roughly chopped
4 ripe tomatoes, roughly chopped
2 tsp small capers, drained
250g pouch ready-cooked Puy lentils
2 tbsp extra-virgin olive oil, plus extra to drizzle
8 slices prosciutto
meat from 2 cooked chicken breasts, torn into pieces
100g bag wild rocket leaves

1 Put the onion in a bowl, drizzle over the vinegar, then season with salt and black pepper. Set aside for 10 minutes or so until the onion has softened slightly.

2 Meanwhile, in another large bowl, mix the parsley and tomatoes with the capers.

3 When ready to serve, tip the lentils into a sieve and rinse with boiling water from the kettle. Drain. Toss the onions and their juices with the lentils, then add the oil and carefully mix everything together. Scoop this on to a large serving platter, and top with the prosciutto, chicken and rocket. Drizzle with more oil and a little more vinegar, if you like, then serve.

PER SERVING 320 kcals, protein 35g, carbs 20g, fat 12g, sat fat 3g, fibre 7g, sugar 5g, salt 2.3g

Storecupboard pasta salad

This salad makes a quick and healthy lunch from leftover cooked pasta and is perfect for a picnic or for the kids' lunchboxes.

TAKES 5 MINUTES • SERVES 2

2 tsp finely chopped red onion
1 tsp capers
1 tbsp pesto
2 tsp olive oil
185g can tuna in spring water, drained
100g/4oz cooked pasta shapes
3 sun-dried tomatoes, chopped

1 Combine the onion, capers, pesto and oil in a small bowl.
2 Flake the tuna into a serving bowl with the pasta and tomatoes, then stir in the pesto mix.

PER SERVING 189 kcals, protein 19g, carbs 12g, fat 7g, sat fat 2g, fibre 2g, sugar 2g, salt 0.91g

Sardines with Sicilian fennel salad

Seasoning sardines with coarse rock salt stops them sticking to the barbecue
(or griddle pan, if the weather does its worst).

TAKES 30 MINUTES • SERVES 2

zest and juice of 1 lemon
bunch of flat-leaf parsley, ½ the leaves
   kept whole, ½ finely chopped
1 small garlic clove, finely chopped
1 fennel bulb, with fronds
50g/2oz toasted pine nuts
50g/2oz raisins
handful of green olives, chopped
3 tbsp olive oil, plus extra to drizzle
4 large sardines, scaled and gutted
a little coarse rock salt, to season

1 Mix together the lemon zest, chopped parsley and garlic, and set aside.

2 Pick the fronds from the fennel and set aside. Halve the fennel bulb and finely slice it. Make the salad by combining the sliced fennel and fronds with the pine nuts, raisins, olives and whole parsley leaves. Dress by drizzling with the oil and lemon juice.

3 Heat a griddle pan or barbecue. Season the fish with rock salt and cook for 2–3 minutes on each side until the eyes turn white. Sprinkle the fish with the parsley mix and lift it on to plates. Drizzle with oil and serve with the fennel salad.

PER SERVING 663 kcals, protein 34g, carbs 20g, fat 50g, sat fat 7g, fibre 3g, sugar 20g, salt 1.49g

Rustic courgette, pine nut & ricotta tart

This rustic tart has been simplified by making it straight on a baking sheet, without using a tart tin.

TAKES 1 HOUR • SERVES 6

2 tbsp olive oil
4 courgettes, thinly sliced (try to use a mixture of different varieties, if you can find them)
2 × 250g tubs ricotta
4 eggs
large handful of basil leaves, shredded
grating of nutmeg
50g/2oz Parmesan, grated
1 large garlic clove, crushed
500g pack puff pastry
flour, for dusting
large handful of pine nuts

1 Heat oven to 200C/180C fan/gas 6. Heat half the oil in a frying pan and sizzle the courgettes for 5 minutes until golden around the edges, then set aside. In a bowl, beat the ricotta with the eggs, basil, nutmeg, half the Parmesan and the garlic.

2 Roll out the pastry on a lightly floured surface to a rough round about 40cm wide, then transfer to a baking sheet. Spread the pastry with the ricotta mix, leaving a 4cm border. Press the courgette slices into the ricotta, then scatter over the pine nuts and remaining Parmesan. Bring the sides up over the edge of the ricotta, pinch to encase the filling, then bake for 30 minutes until the filling is puffed up and golden. Leave to cool slightly and enjoy warm or cold with a crisp green salad.

PER SERVING 620 kcals, protein 24g, carbs 36g, fat 43g, sat fat 17g, fibre 1g, sugar 5g, salt 1.17g

Winter minestrone with pesto croûtes

The Italian trinity of onion, carrot and celery (called soffritto*) gives this soup its heart, then add what you will. Instead of cabbage, you could use kale, spinach or broccoli.*

TAKES 55 MINUTES • SERVES 4

2 tbsp olive oil
1 onion, chopped
100g/4oz unsmoked lardons or
    chopped streaky bacon
2 large carrots, chopped
2 celery sticks, chopped
1 medium potato, chopped
2 garlic cloves, finely chopped or
    crushed
400g can chopped tomatoes
1 litre/1¾ pints vegetable stock (from
    granules or a cube)
2 tsp chopped sage leaves or 1 tsp
    dried
few cabbage leaves, shredded
400g can haricot beans
handful of chopped flat-leaf parsley

FOR THE PESTO CROUTES

3–4 slices crusty bread
3 tbsp olive oil
1 tbsp pesto

1 Heat the oil in a large pan, add the onion and lardons or bacon, and fry for about 5 minutes until the onion is starting to brown. Tip in the carrots, celery, potato and garlic, stir well and cook for a few minutes.

2 Add the tomatoes, stock and sage, and bring to the boil, stirring. Reduce the heat to a simmer and cook, partly covered, for 30 minutes, stirring in the cabbage after 15 minutes.

3 Meanwhile, make the croûtes. Cut the bread into chunks, about 2cm thick. Tip into an ovenproof pan. Mix the oil and pesto in a bowl, then add to the bread, tossing the mixture with your hands until the croûtes are evenly coated. Bake in a moderate oven for about 10 minutes until crisp.

4 Drain and rinse the beans, and add to the soup with the parsley. Season and serve topped with the croûtes.

PER SERVING 447 kcals, protein 17g, carbs 45g, fat 23g, sat fat 5g, fibre 9g, sugar 12g, salt 4.29g

Roasted tomato, basil & Parmesan tart

Look out for all-butter pastry, which has more of a homemade flavour. Roasting the tomatoes beforehand intensifies their taste and stops things getting soggy.

TAKES ABOUT 1 HOUR 20 MINUTES,
PLUS CHILLING • SERVES 8

500g pack ready-made shortcrust
  pastry
plain flour, to dust
300g/10oz cherry tomatoes
drizzle of olive oil
2 eggs
284ml pot double cream
handful of basil leaves, shredded,
  plus a few small ones left whole
  to garnish
50g/2oz Parmesan, grated

1 Heat oven to 200C/180C fan/gas 6. Roll out the pastry on a lightly floured surface then use to line a 25cm tart tin. Chill for 20 minutes.
2 In a small roasting tin, drizzle the tomatoes with oil and season. Put the tomatoes on a low shelf in the oven.
3 Lightly prick the pastry base with a fork, line the tart case with baking parchment, then fill with baking beans. Bake for 20 minutes then remove from the oven (take out the tomatoes at the same time), take off the paper and beans, and return the pastry case to the oven for 5–10 minutes more until biscuit brown.
4 Beat together the eggs, cream, basil and seasoning. Scatter the tomatoes and half the cheese over the case, then pour over the cream mixture. Sprinkle with remaining cheese. Bake for 20–25 minutes until set and golden. Cool in the tin, trim, if you like, then serve garnished with the remaining basil.

PER SERVING 494 kcals, protein 9g, carbs 29g, fat 39g, sat fat 22g, fibre 2g, sugar 2g, salt 0.48g

Simple squash risotto

Not content with adding roasted squash to this risotto, we've stirred mashed squash through the rice, too, giving extra flavour and, of course, that fabulous golden colour.

TAKES ABOUT 50 MINUTES

● **SERVES 2**

1 butternut squash, peeled, deseeded
   and cut into 2cm/¾in cubes
4 tbsp light olive oil
600ml/1 pint vegetable stock
1 small onion, finely chopped
50g/2oz unsalted butter
1 celery stick, finely chopped
2 garlic cloves, crushed
1 bay leaf
1 tsp thyme leaves
140g/5oz risotto rice
100ml/3½fl oz white wine
50g/2oz Parmesan, finely grated

1 Heat oven to 200C/180C fan/gas 6. Toss half the squash in half the oil, season, then roast for 30 minutes. Heat the stock and remaining squash in a small pan; keep it simmering.

2 Meanwhile, fry the onion in the remaining oil and half the butter for 3 minutes. Stir in the celery, garlic and herbs. Cover, cook for 2 minutes, then stir in the rice. Cook, uncovered, for a further 5 minutes, stirring constantly.

3 Turn up the heat, stir in the wine and let it reduce. Reduce the heat then add the hot stock one ladle at a time, stirring each ladleful until absorbed. When you only have a little stock left, mash it with the poached squash and stir the mixture into the risotto.

4 Turn off the heat and dot with the remaining butter and most of the cheese. Cover for 2 minutes, then stir, season and serve with the roast squash and remaining Parmesan.

PER SERVING 864 kcals, protein 19g, carbs 83g, fat 51g, sat fat 21g, fibre 7g, sugar 17g, salt 0.94g

Italian turkey steaks with garlicky bean mash

The secret to cooking tasty turkey is to keep it moist. Make sure your pan is hot but not smoking, then brown the steaks quickly and finish in the oven.

TAKES 20 MINUTES • SERVES 4

zest of 2 lemons, juice from 1½
3 tbsp olive oil
3 garlic cloves, crushed
2 tsp chopped fresh oregano, or 1 tsp dried
4 thick turkey steaks
250g punnet cherry or small plum tomatoes, some halved, some left whole
750g bag frozen broad beans

1 Heat oven to 200C/180C fan/gas 6 and bring a pan of water to the boil. Mix most of the lemon zest with the lemon juice, oil and garlic, and season. Set aside two-thirds of this dressing. Add the oregano to the remaining third, tip this on to a plate and turn the turkey steaks in it to coat.

2 Brown the turkey in a non-stick frying pan for 1–2 minutes, then transfer to a roasting tin. Scatter the tomatoes around, then roast in the oven for 4–8 minutes, depending on the thickness of the turkey steaks, until just cooked through.

3 Meanwhile, boil the beans for 4–5 minutes until tender. Tip a ladle of the cooking water into a food processor, drain the beans, then add the beans to the processor with the reserved lemon dressing. Whizz to a mash, then serve topped with a turkey steak, the remaining lemon zest and the juicy tomatoes alongside.

PER SERVING 357 kcals, protein 48g, carbs 16g, fat 12g, sat fat 2g, fibre 12g, sugar 7g, salt 0.22g

Chicken with tomato & olives

A great way to use up leftovers from a roast, all this needs is some crusty bread to mop up the juices. The sauce would be good with prawns too.

TAKES 25 MINUTES ● SERVES 4

20g pack basil
2 tbsp oil
2 garlic cloves, finely sliced
2 × 400g cans cherry tomatoes
1 tsp caster sugar
handful of olives (green or black)
400g/14oz cooked chicken
crusty bread, to serve

1 Finely chop the stalks from the basil and shred most of the leaves. Heat the oil in a medium frying pan, then soften the garlic and basil stalks for around 3 minutes. Tip in the tomatoes, sugar and the shredded basil leaves. Bring to a boil, then simmer for 15 minutes until reduced and saucy. Season.

2 Stir in the olives, then the chicken and warm through for a couple of minutes. Scatter with the remaining whole basil leaves then serve with crusty bread.

PER SERVING (inc skin) 531 kcals, protein 52g, carbs 8g, fat 32g, sat fat 9g, fibre 2g, sugar 7g, salt 1.4g

Gnocchi with creamy tomato & spinach sauce

Gnocchi – small potato dumplings – are popular in northern Italy. You could also try tossing this sauce through pasta.

TAKES 20 MINUTES ● SERVES 4

1 tbsp olive oil
2 garlic cloves, crushed
400g can chopped tomatoes
140g/5oz mascarpone
500g pack gnocchi
200g bag baby leaf spinach
handful of basil leaves and Parmesan
    shavings, to garnish (optional)

1 Heat the oil in a frying pan and fry the garlic until golden. Add the tomatoes, season, then simmer for 10 minutes. Stir in the mascarpone and cook for 2 minutes more.

2 Meanwhile, boil the gnocchi according to the packet instructions. Add the spinach for the final minute of cooking. Drain well, pour back into the pan, then stir the sauce through. Mix well and serve immediately with basil leaves and Parmesan shavings scattered over, if you like.

PER SERVING 393 kcals, protein 9g, carbs 48g, fat 20g, sat fat 11g, fibre 4g, sugar 7g, salt 1.67g

Italian-style chicken burger & chips

Bring a little Italian flavour to a weeknight classic. Ready-cooked polenta, made from cornmeal, is available in shrink-wrapped packs in most supermarkets.

TAKES 30 MINUTES ● SERVES 4

500g pack ready-cooked polenta
2 tbsp olive oil
2 chicken breasts
25g/1oz dried breadcrumbs
25g/1oz Parmesan
125g ball mozzarella, sliced
4 burger or ciabatta buns, lightly
    toasted
salad leaves, sun-blushed tomatoes
    and fresh basil pesto, to serve

1 Heat oven to 200C/180C fan/gas 6. Cut the polenta into thick chips and rub them all over with a little oil. Spread out over a baking sheet and cook for around 20 minutes until golden.

2 Cut each chicken breast in half, lightly flatten using a rolling pin or heavy can, then rub all over with more of the oil. Spread out the breadcrumbs and Parmesan on a plate then dip in the chicken to coat.

3 Put the chicken breasts on another baking sheet and cook for 10–12 minutes until just crisp and cooked through. Place the mozzarella on top and return to the oven until starting to melt.

4 Pile the burgers on to buns with some salad leaves, the tomatoes and a dollop of pesto. Serve with the polenta chips.

PER SERVING 495 kcals, protein 33g, carbs 54g, fat 18g, sat fat 7g, fibre 4g, sugar 4g, salt 2.08g

Chicken saltimbocca with basil mash

Wrapping chicken in prosciutto keeps it beautifully moist as it cooks. You could use thin-cut bacon for this smart supper instead, if you prefer.

TAKES 35 MINUTES • SERVES 2

2 skinless chicken breast fillets
2 large basil leaves
2 slices prosciutto
1 tbsp olive oil
2 tbsp Marsala
100ml/3½fl oz chicken stock

FOR THE BASIL MASH

500g/1lb 2oz potatoes, peeled and
    cut into large chunks
2–3 tbsp milk
1 tbsp grated Parmesan
1–2 tbsp chopped basil leaves

1 First, make the mash. Boil the potatoes in a pan of salted water for around 15–20 minutes until tender. Drain, mash, then stir in the milk, Parmesan and basil. Season and keep warm.

2 Meanwhile, sit the chicken breasts on a board and cut through them horizontally, leaving one side attached. Open them up like a book, lay a basil leaf on top of each, then top with a slice of prosciutto. Secure with a cocktail stick.

3 Heat the oil in a large, non-stick frying pan and add the chicken breasts, ham-side down. Cook for 2–3 minutes until golden, then turn and cook for 2 minutes more. Pour over the Marsala and bubble for 1 minute. Add the stock then simmer for 5 minutes until the chicken is cooked. Lift out the chicken, keep warm, then bubble the pan juices a little until syrupy. Serve alongside the basil mash.

PER SERVING 481 kcals, protein 47g, carbs 50g, fat 11g, sat fat 3g, fibre 4g, sugar 4g, salt 1.2g

Rosemary roast lamb chops & potatoes

Cooked in just one pan this quick lamb is ideal for a weeknight, or perhaps a summer Sunday. Try this recipe with juicy pork chops or chicken breasts too.

TAKES 40 MINUTES ● SERVES 4

3 tbsp olive oil
8 lamb chops
1kg/2lb 4oz potatoes, chopped into small chunks
4 rosemary sprigs
4 garlic cloves, left whole
250g/9oz cherry tomatoes
1 tbsp balsamic vinegar

1 Heat oven to 220C/200C fan/gas 7. Heat half the oil in a flameproof roasting tin or ovenproof sauté pan. Brown the chops for 2 minutes on each side, then lift them out of the pan. Add the rest of the oil, throw in the potatoes, then fry them for 4–5 minutes until starting to brown. Toss in the rosemary and garlic, then nestle the lamb in among the fried potatoes.
2 Roast everything together for around 20 minutes, then scatter over the tomatoes and drizzle with the vinegar. Return to the oven for 5 minutes more until the tomatoes just begin to split. Serve straight from the dish.

PER SERVING 754 kcals, protein 36g, carbs 46g, fat 48g, sat fat 21g, fibre 4g, sugar 4g, salt 0.34g

Smoked salmon & lemon risotto

Smoked salmon might sound expensive for midweek cooking, but it is no more costly than red meat. Look out for salmon trimmings, which are more economical than slices.

TAKES 25 MINUTES ● SERVES 4

2 tbsp olive oil
1 onion, finely chopped
350g/12oz risotto rice, such as arborio
1 garlic clove, finely chopped
1.5 litres/2¾ pints boiling vegetable
   stock
170g pack smoked salmon, three-
   quarters chopped
85g/3oz reduced-fat mascarpone
3 tbsp flat-leaf parsley, chopped
zest of 1 lemon, plus a squeeze of the
   juice (optional)
handful of rocket leaves

1 Fry the onion gently in the oil for 5 minutes until softened. Add the rice and garlic, then cook for 2 minutes, stirring continuously. Add a third of the stock, then simmer and stir until it has all been absorbed. Repeat twice until the rice is cooked and creamy. The whole process should take about 20 minutes.

2 Remove from the heat and add the chopped salmon, mascarpone, parsley and lemon zest. Season with black pepper, but don't add salt as the salmon will be salty enough. Leave for 5 minutes to settle, then taste and add a little lemon juice, if you like. Serve topped with the reserved salmon (roughly torn) and the rocket.

PER SERVING 500 kcals, protein 21g, carbs 75g, fat 15g, sat fat 5g, fibre 4g, sugar 5g, salt 2.58g

Meatballs with pesto mash

If you're really pushed for time, pick up a packet of fresh meatballs and fry them off as below. Stir a little more basil through the sauce to pep up the flavour.

TAKES 30 MINUTES ● SERVES 4

400g/14oz lean minced beef
small bunch of basil, most leaves
    roughly chopped, reserving a few
    whole to garnish
1 tbsp Worcestershire sauce
1 tsp olive oil
½ × 700g bottle passata with onions
    and garlic
1kg/2lb 4oz potatoes, peeled and cut
    into small chunks
150ml/¼ pint milk
2 tbsp fresh basil pesto

1 Mix the mince with half the chopped basil, the Worcestershire sauce and some seasoning, then use your hands to shape into 16 meatballs. Heat a non-stick frying pan, add the oil, then fry the meatballs for 5 minutes, turning them until they are browned all over. Tip in the passata and remaining chopped basil. Simmer gently for 10 minutes until the meatballs are cooked through.

2 Meanwhile, boil the potatoes in a pan for 10–15 minutes until tender. Drain well, then return to the pan over a low heat and mash – leaving the heat on will help to dry out the potatoes for a fluffier mash. Stir in the milk, then marble through the pesto. Pile the mash on to four plates, spoon over the meatballs and some sauce, and serve scattered with the reserved basil.

PER SERVING 438 kcals, protein 31g, carbs 51g, fat 14g, sat fat 6g, fibre 4g, sugar 7g, salt 0.96g

Chicken, fennel & tomato ragout

This bold one pot is bursting with Mediterranean flavours and no less than four of your 5-a-day. The fennel loses its crunch and gains a melting sweetness as it cooks.

TAKES 35 MINUTES ● **SERVES 2**

1 large fennel bulb
1 tbsp olive oil
2 boneless skinless chicken breasts, cut into chunks
1 garlic clove, chopped
200g/8oz new potatoes, cut into chunks
400g can chopped tomatoes
150ml/¼ pint chicken or vegetable stock
3 roasted red peppers in brine, from a jar or deli counter, drained and chopped
crusty bread, to serve

1 Trim the green fronds from the fennel and reserve. Halve then quarter the fennel, cut out the core and discard, then cut the fennel lengthways into slices. Heat the oil in a pan, add the chicken, then fry quickly until lightly coloured. Add the fennel and garlic, then stir briefly until the fennel is glistening.

2 Tip in the potatoes, tomatoes, stock and a little seasoning, and bring to the boil. Cover and simmer for 20 minutes until the potatoes are tender. Stir in the peppers and heat through. Roughly chop the reserved fennel fronds, then sprinkle over the ragout. Serve with crusty bread for mopping up the juices.

PER SERVING 351 kcals, protein 42g, carbs 28g, fat 9g, sat fat 1g, fibre 6g, sugar 10g, salt 1.43g

Lamb steaks with tomatoes & olives

This clever dish makes its own delicious sauce, ready for mopping up with crusty bread or mashed potatoes.

TAKES 25 MINUTES ● **SERVES 4**

2 tbsp olive oil

4 lamb leg steaks (about 140g/5oz each)

1 large red onion, cut into 8 wedges

2 tsp dried oregano

150ml/¼ pint white wine

400g pack cherry tomatoes

100g/4oz black olives

handful of flat-leaf parsley, chopped, to garnish

1 Heat oven to 200C/180C fan/gas 6. Heat the oil in a large roasting tin on the hob. Brown the lamb steaks in the tin over a high heat for about 1 minute each side.

2 Add the onion to the roasting tin with the oregano. Pour over the wine and throw in the tomatoes. Scatter the olives over the top, then place the tin in the oven for 15 minutes until the lamb is cooked. Scatter with parsley and serve.

PER SERVING 322 kcals, protein 21g, carbs 7g, fat 21g, sat fat 7g, fibre 2g, sugar 6g, salt 1.84g

Roasted fish Italian-style

Make sure that you choose thick fillets of fish so that the flesh stays moist in the middle – some sustainably caught cod, haddock or hake would do nicely.

TAKES 25 MINUTES • SERVES 4

4 firm white fish fillets, skin on
1 tbsp olive oil
500g/1lb 2oz cherry tomatoes, halved
50g/2oz pitted black olives
25g/1oz pine nuts
large handful of basil leaves, to garnish
extra-virgin olive oil, to drizzle

1 Heat oven to 200C/180C fan/gas 6. Season the fish. Heat the oil in a large pan then cook the fillets, skin-side down, for 2–3 minutes until just crisp. Transfer to a large roasting tin, skin-side down. Scatter the tomatoes, olives and pine nuts around the fillets then season to taste.

2 Put the tin in the oven and roast for 12–15 minutes until the fish is tender. Remove from the oven and scatter the basil leaves over the tomatoes. Spoon the tomatoes on to four warm plates and top each pile with a fish fillet. Drizzle with a little extra-virgin olive oil to serve.

PER SERVING 322 kcals, protein 28g, carbs 4g, fat 22g, sat fat 3g, fibre 2g, sugar 4g, salt 0.45g

Oven-baked porcini & thyme risotto

If you're not the risotto-stirring type, try this easy oven-baked recipe – the result is still creamy and comforting, and smart enough to share with friends.

TAKES 45 MINUTES • SERVES 4

25g pack dried porcini mushrooms
2 tbsp olive oil
1 small onion, finely chopped
2 garlic cloves, crushed
2 tsp thyme leaves, plus extra to
    garnish
350g/12oz risotto rice (carnaroli is
    ideal)
750ml/1¼ pints hot vegetable stock
100ml/3½fl oz white wine
handful of grated Parmesan, plus
    shavings, to garnish

1 Put the mushrooms in a bowl, pour over 425ml/¾ pint boiling water and leave to soak for 10 minutes. Meanwhile, heat the oil in an ovenproof pan and fry the onion for 2 minutes until starting to soften. Add the garlic and cook for another minute.

2 Heat oven to 190C/170C fan/gas 5. Lift the mushrooms from the the liquid and chop, reserving the liquid. Add the mushrooms, thyme and rice to the onion in the pan, then stir well. Strain over the mushroom liquid as it can be gritty, pour in the stock and wine and bring to the boil.

3 Season to taste, cover and bake for 25 minutes or until the rice is just cooked and all the liquid has been absorbed. Stir in the grated Parmesan, check the seasoning, and serve sprinkled with the extra thyme leaves and the Parmesan shavings, if you like.

PER SERVING 374 kcals, protein 9g, carbs 75g, fat 6g, sat fat 1g, fibre 2g, sugar 5g, salt 0.64g

Turkey meatballs in tomato & fennel sauce

This quick, tasty and economical supper is a healthy way of getting the family fed. Switch the fennel seeds for a pinch of dried dill, if you prefer.

TAKES ABOUT 40 MINUTES
● **SERVES 4**

400g/14oz minced turkey
25g/1oz fresh white breadcrumbs
2 garlic cloves, crushed
2 tbsp olive oil
1 onion, chopped
1 carrot, diced
1 tsp fennel seeds
400g can chopped tomatoes
1 tbsp tomato purée
400g/14oz spaghetti, cooked, to serve
a little grated Parmesan, to serve

1 Put the mince in a mixing bowl with the breadcrumbs and half the garlic. Season and mix well to combine. Using your hands, shape the mixture into 12 balls then chill for 10 minutes.

2 Meanwhile, heat 1 tablespoon of the oil in a pan. Add the onion, carrot and remaining garlic, and cook for 5–6 minutes until softened. Add the fennel seeds and cook for a few seconds. Tip in the tomatoes with half a can of water then stir in the tomato purée. Season and simmer for 15 minutes until thickened. Using an electric hand blender, whizz to a chunky sauce.

3 Meanwhile, heat the remaining oil in a non-stick frying pan and fry the meatballs for 8–10 minutes until cooked through. Transfer to the sauce and simmer until piping hot. Serve spooned over the spaghetti and some grated Parmesan for sprinkling, if you like.

PER SERVING 216 kcals, protein 26g, carbs 12g, fat 8g, sat fat 1g, fibre 2g, sugar 6g, salt 0.46

Herb-crusted fish

A superhealthy way to enjoy fish, made with storecupboard ingredients. Mayonnaise acts as a great 'glue' for the crumbs, and bastes the fish as it cooks.

TAKES 25 MINUTES • SERVES 4

1 tbsp olive oil, plus extra for greasing and drizzling

4 skinless chunky sustainably caught white fish fillets, about 140g/5oz each

2 handfuls of cherry tomatoes

3 tbsp mayonnaise

1 tsp garlic paste or 1 garlic clove, crushed

100g/4oz white breadcrumbs (about 5 slices white bread)

zest and juice of 1 lemon

2 handfuls of flat-leaf parsley, leaves roughly chopped

1 Heat oven to 220C/200C fan/gas 7. Lightly oil a large baking sheet then lay the fish and tomatoes alongside each other. In a small bowl, mix the mayonnaise with the garlic paste or crushed garlic, then spread evenly over the fish.

2 In a separate bowl, toss together the breadcrumbs, lemon zest, juice and parsley, then season to taste. Top the fish with the breadcrumb mixture. Drizzle a little oil over the fish and tomatoes, then bake for 15 minutes or until the fish flakes slightly when pressed and the crust is golden and crunchy.

PER SERVING 324 kcals, protein 30g, carbs 21g, fat 14g, sat fat 2g, fibre 1g, sugar 2g, salt 0.87g

One-pan baked chicken with squash, sage & walnuts

A simple supper full of soft sticky vegetables and tender, golden chicken. Serve with creamy mashed potatoes and perhaps a leafy salad.

TAKES 1 HOUR 20 MINUTES

- **SERVES 4**

1kg/2lb 4oz mixed chicken thigh and drumstick pieces

3 tbsp olive oil

3 red onions, peeled and cut into large wedges

1 butternut squash, peeled, deseeded and cut into wedges

bunch of sage, leaves picked

100g/4oz walnut halves, very roughly chopped

good splash of balsamic or sherry vinegar

1 Heat oven to 220C/200C fan/gas 7. Tip the chicken pieces into a large roasting tin and toss with the oil, onions and squash. Season with salt and black pepper and arrange the chicken so it is skin-side up.

2 Roast for about 25 minutes in the oven, remove, toss through the sage and walnuts then drizzle over the vinegar. Using tongs, again arrange the chicken so it is all skin-side up. Roast for another 25–30 minutes until the chicken is golden brown and the veg soft and sticky. Serve straight from the tin.

PER SERVING 573 kcals, protein 27g, carbs 23g, fat 42g, sat fat 8g, fibre 5g, sugar 13g, salt 0.27g

Tomato & mozzarella spaghetti bake

Creamy mozzarella and a quick tomato sauce turn simple spaghetti into an oozy pasta bake that everyone will love. Serve with a fresh green salad.

TAKES 45 MINUTES • SERVES 4

2 tbsp olive oil
2 garlic cloves, chopped
2 × 400g cans chopped tomatoes
good pinch of chilli powder
400g/14oz spaghetti, broken into short lengths
handful of basil leaves, plus a few extra to garnish
250g pack mozzarella, sliced
50g/2oz grated Parmesan

1 Heat oven to 200C/180C fan/gas 6. Heat the oil in large pan, add the garlic and fry for 1 minute. Add the tomatoes, chilli and seasoning, bring to the boil, then simmer for 10 minutes.

2 Meanwhile, cook the spaghetti according to the packet instructions, then drain. Mix the spaghetti with the tomato sauce and basil, then spoon half into a large ovenproof dish. Arrange half the mozzarella over the top and sprinkle with half the Parmesan. Repeat the layers, then bake for 15–20 minutes until lightly browned on top. Scatter with extra basil and serve.

PER SERVING 639 kcals, protein 31g, carbs 80g, fat 24g, sat fat 11g, fibre 5g, sugar 8g, salt 1.14g

Spaghetti with spinach & garlic

Remember that wholewheat pasta absorbs a lot more sauce than white pasta, so always keep some cooking water aside to loosen it a little.

TAKES 20 MINUTES • SERVES 4

500g pack wholewheat spaghetti
500g/1lb 2oz baby leaf spinach
3 tbsp olive oil, plus extra to drizzle
4 garlic cloves, finely sliced
2 tbsp red wine vinegar
handful of pine nuts
50g/2oz Parmesan, half grated, half shaved
chilli flakes, to garnish

1 Cook the spaghetti according to the packet instructions. Meanwhile, boil the kettle and tip the spinach into a large colander. Pour over boiling water until it's completely wilted (you may need two kettles of water), then cool under cold water and press the spinach into a ball, squeezing out all the water. Roughly chop the spinach and set aside.

2 Very gently, heat the oil and cook the garlic in a small pan for a few minutes until it just starts to brown, then add the vinegar. Bubble for 1 minute then turn off the heat.

3 When the spaghetti is cooked, reserve some of the water, then drain. In a large bowl, toss the spaghetti with the garlicky oil, spinach, pine nuts and the grated Parmesan. Add enough water to loosen everything. Serve in bowls along with the Parmesan shavings and chilli flakes, plus more oil for drizzling.

PER SERVING 549 kcals, protein 21g, carbs 86g, fat 16g, sat fat 2g, fibre 13g, sugar 7g, salt 0.86g

Fuss-free lasagne

When you're taking the time to make lasagne properly, it's worth making double and stashing one in the freezer for another day, so this recipe will make two lasagnes.

TAKES ABOUT 2 HOURS • SERVES 10

3 tbsp olive oil
4 onions, finely chopped
8 garlic cloves, crushed
1 tbsp dried mixed herbs
2 bay leaves
1kg/2lb 4oz minced beef
4 × 400g cans chopped tomatoes
4 tbsp tomato ketchup
small glass of red wine
200g/8oz butter
140g/5oz plain flour
1.7 litres/3 pints milk
few gratings of nutmeg
250g mozzarella, grated
18–20 no-cook lasagne sheets
85g/3oz Parmesan, grated

1 Heat the oil in a large pan then cook the onions for 10 minutes. Add the garlic, herbs and bay leaves; cook for 2 minutes more. Tip into a bowl. Brown the beef in four batches, adding each to the onions once cooked. Return everything to the pan, then tip in the tomatoes, ketchup and red wine. Simmer for 30 minutes.
2 For the white sauce, tip the butter, flour, milk and nutmeg into a pan, season, then bring to a simmer, whisking. Simmer for 5 minutes, whisking, until smooth and thickened.
3 Place a thin layer of meat sauce in the bottom of two ovenproof baking dishes, drizzle with a little white sauce then scatter with some mozzarella. Cover with a few lasagne sheets, top with more of both sauces, more mozzarella and pasta. Repeat, then top with white sauce and Parmesan.
4 Heat oven to 200C/180C fan/gas 6 and cook for 35–40 minutes, until golden.

PER SERVING 847 kcals, protein 43g, carbs 65g, fat 48g, sat fat 25g, fibre 5g, sugar 17g, salt 1.58g

Pasta with creamy walnut pesto

Pine nuts are often used to make sauces in Italy, but here walnuts are added to give wonderful depth of flavour to a creamy pesto.

TAKES 25 MINUTES • SERVES 4

400g/14oz pasta (orecchiette is ideal, but any shape will do)
175g/6oz walnut halves or pieces
1 garlic clove
handful of fresh basil, leaves roughly torn, plus extra to garnish (optional)
100g/4oz Parmesan, freshly grated, plus extra to sprinkle (optional)
50g/2oz butter
4 tbsp extra-virgin olive oil
50ml/2fl oz double cream

1 Cook the pasta according to the packet instructions. Meanwhile, put the walnuts and garlic in a food processor, and whizz until finely chopped. Add the basil, cheese, butter and oil, and pulse the pesto a few more times. Season.
2 Pour the cream into a pan and warm it through. Add two-thirds of the pesto to the cream, then gently heat to loosen it. When the pasta is ready, drain, reserving 2 tablespoons of the cooking water, then mix both with the sauce. Serve immediately, sprinkled with the extra Parmesan and basil, if using. The leftover pesto will keep in an airtight container in the fridge for up to a week or can be frozen for up to a month.

PER SERVING 805 kcals, protein 23g, carbs 77g, fat 47g, sat fat 15g, fibre 4g, sugar 3g, salt 0.48g

Spicy tuna pasta

Here's a way to spice up the classic combination of tuna and pasta. Perhaps surprisingly, ordinary canned tuna is easily shaped into 'meatballs'.

TAKES 25 MINUTES ● **SERVES 4**

2 × 185g cans tuna in spring water, drained
2 spring onions, chopped
1 egg, beaten
1 tbsp vegetable oil
350g jar tomato and chilli sauce (or see page 94 for a basic sauce recipe, adding a pinch of dried chilli)
½ × 70g bag rocket leaves, roughly chopped
400g/14oz spaghetti

1 Squeeze the excess water from the tuna, put the fish in a bowl with the spring onions and egg, then stir together. Use your hands to shape the mixture into small walnut-sized balls – it should make about 12.

2 Heat the oil in a large non-stick frying pan, tip in the tuna balls, then cook for 5–10 minutes until golden all over. Pour over the tomato and chilli sauce, then cook for 5 minutes more, adding a little boiling water if the sauce looks dry.

3 Meanwhile, cook the pasta according to the packet instructions, then drain. Stir through the sauce and most of the rocket. Serve in bowls with the tuna balls and the remaining rocket on top.

PER SERVING 552 kcals, protein 33g, carbs 81g, fat 13g, sat fat 2g, fibre 4g, sugar 9g, salt 1.16g

Bacon, pea & basil macaroni

This family-friendly bake uses plenty of veg and some soft cheese – something
perhaps more likely to be in the fridge than a pot of cream or crème fraiche.

TAKES 30 MINUTES • SERVES 4

6 rashers streaky bacon, chopped
2 leeks, finely sliced into rings
1 tbsp vegetable oil
140g/5oz frozen peas
400g/14oz macaroni
200g pack soft cheese
85g/3oz mature Cheddar, grated
1 tsp English mustard
small bunch of basil leaves, shredded

1 In a wide pan, fry the bacon and leeks in the oil for 10 minutes until the bacon is golden and the leeks soft. Tip in the peas and heat through. Meanwhile, cook the pasta according to the packet instructions and heat the grill to high.
2 Reserve 150ml/¼ pint of the cooking water before you drain the pasta, then add the reserved water to the bacon and veg with the soft cheese, half the grated cheese and all of the mustard. Stir until the cheese melts into a creamy sauce. Stir in most of the basil and the pasta, then scatter with the remaining cheese. Grill for 2–3 minutes until the cheese melts. Serve scattered with the remaining basil.

PER SERVING 703 kcals, protein 28g, carbs 81g, fat 32g, sat fat 16g, fibre 6g, sugar 7g, salt 1.87g

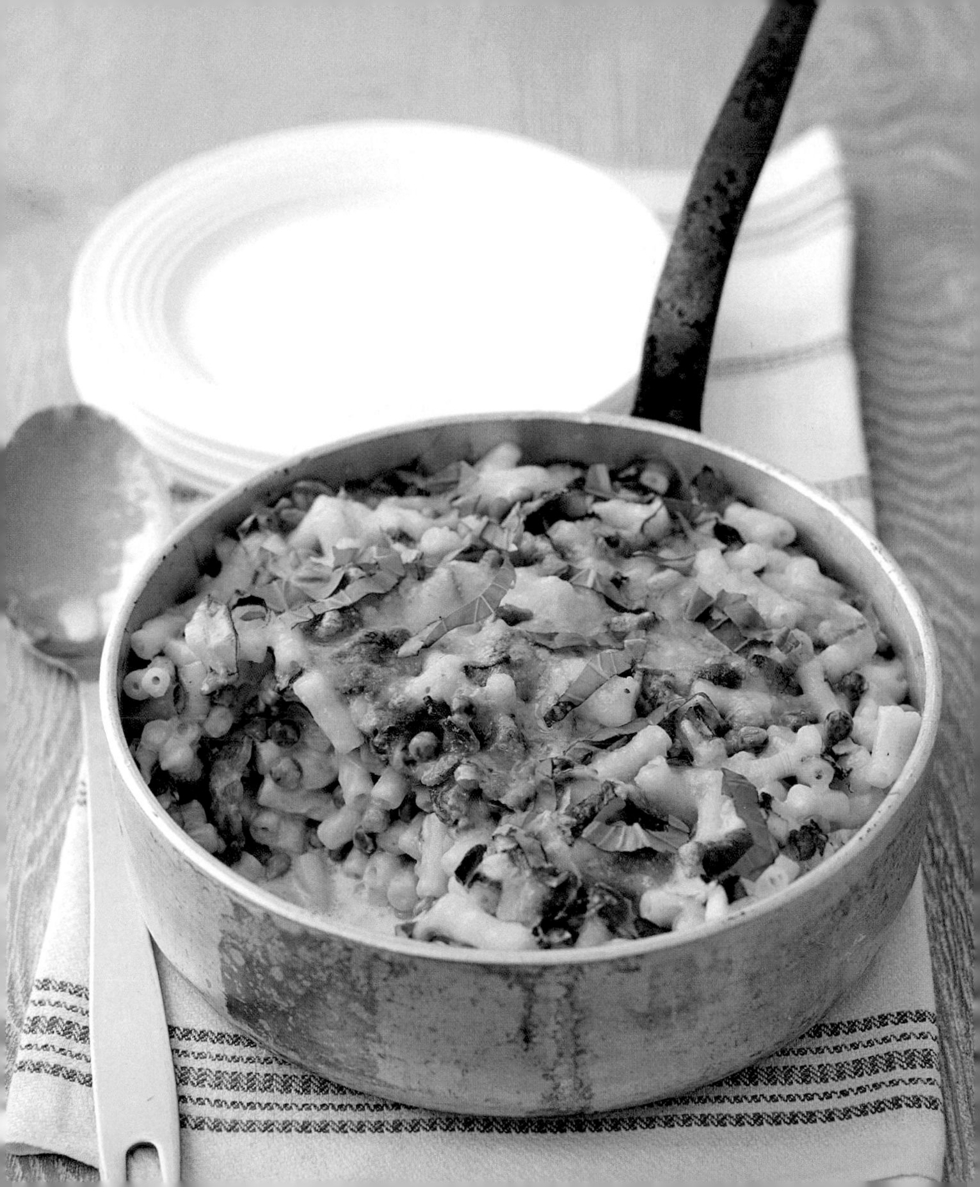

Spaghetti carbonara

Adding a little cream to this simple supper is a luxurious twist, but not essential: use three whole eggs plus one yolk instead.

TAKES 20 MINUTES • SERVES 4

400g/14oz spaghetti
1 tbsp olive oil
200g/8oz smoked pancetta cubes or
    chopped streaky bacon
2 eggs, plus 1 egg yolk
½ × 142ml pot double cream
50g/2oz Grana Padano or Parmesan,
    finely grated, plus extra to garnish
2 garlic cloves, crushed

1 Cook the pasta according to the packet instructions. Meanwhile, heat the oil in a frying pan. When hot, tip in the pancetta or streaky bacon. Fry over a medium heat until the fat in the meat has melted down into the pan and the meat has turned lightly golden. Remove the pan from the heat and set aside.

2 Beat the eggs and the egg yolk with the cream, cheese and some seasoning. Add the garlic to the pancetta and return the frying pan to hob. Fry over a high heat for 1 minute or until the garlic is cooked and the pancetta warmed through. Meanwhile, drain the spaghetti.

3 Tip the pasta back into the hot pan, off the heat. Pour the egg mixture over the pasta, followed by the hot pancetta, garlic and any fat from the pan. Toss quickly and thoroughly with a spaghetti spoon or tongs. The pasta is ready when the eggs have thickened to a smooth, creamy sauce. Serve with extra cheese.

PER SERVING 734 kcals, protein 33g, carbs 75g, fat 36g, sat fat 15g, fibre 3g, sugar 4g, salt 2.95g

Tortellini with ricotta, spinach & bacon

The subtle crunch of toasted walnuts, a bite of lemon and Parmesan and the creaminess of the ricotta make this recipe special enough for summer entertaining.

TAKES 15 MINUTES • SERVES 4

250g pack filled tortellini (we used ricotta and spinach)
2 rashers lean back bacon
25g/1oz walnut pieces
juice of 1 lemon, zest of ½
1 tbsp finely grated Parmesan, plus extra to garnish (optional)
1 tbsp olive oil, plus extra to drizzle (optional)
100g bag baby leaf spinach
2 tbsp ricotta

1 Heat the grill to high. Cook the pasta according to the packet instructions, then tip into a colander and cool under gently running water. Meanwhile, grill the bacon on a baking sheet until golden and crisp at the edges. When almost ready, tip the walnuts on to the sheet to toast them a little. Snip the bacon into small strips.

2 Mix the lemon juice and zest, Parmesan and oil in a large bowl. Season with black pepper, then add the spinach, tortellini, bacon and walnuts. Toss well, add the ricotta in small blobs, then gently toss. Season to taste, then serve with a drizzle more oil and more Parmesan, if you like.

PER SERVING 285 kcals, protein 11g, carbs 30g, fat 14g, sat fat 5g, fibre 2g, sugar 3g, salt 1.13g

Broccoli pesto pasta

A brilliantly healthy and tasty alternative to classic pesto. Try frozen peas instead of broccoli, if that's what you've got in.

TAKES 15–20 MINUTES ● SERVES 4

400g/14oz penne, farfalle or conchiglie
250g/9oz broccoli, cut into small florets
zest of 1 lemon, juice of ½
½ tsp dried chilli flakes
3 tbsp pine nuts
5 tbsp extra-virgin olive oil
3 tbsp Parmesan, grated

1 Cook the pasta according to the packet instructions. Meanwhile, bring a smaller pan of salted water to the boil, add the broccoli and boil for 4 minutes.
2 Drain the broccoli and return it to the pan. Lightly mash the broccoli with a potato masher or fork. Mix in the lemon zest, chilli and pine nuts.
3 Drain the pasta and return it to the pan. Stir in the broccoli pesto and sprinkle with the lemon juice. Pour in the oil and generously season with salt and black pepper. Spoon in the grated Parmesan, toss the pasta well and serve.

PER SERVING 604 kcals, protein 19g, carbs 79g, fat 26g, sat fat 4g, fibre 5g, added sugar none, salt 0.47g

Asparagus cream pasta

Making a cream out of the asparagus stalks saves the taste, and gives every mouthful of pasta a delicious springtime flavour.

TAKES 40 MINUTES • SERVES 2

1 bunch asparagus
142ml pot double cream
2 garlic cloves, peeled, but left whole
50g/2oz Parmesan, half grated, half
   shaved
250g/9oz tagliatelle

1 To prepare the asparagus, cut off and discard the woody ends, then neatly cut the tips away from the stalks. Keep the tips and stalks separate. In a small pan, bring the cream and garlic to the boil. Take off the heat, remove and discard the garlic, then set the pan aside.

2 Cook the asparagus stalks in boiling salted water for about 4–5 minutes until tender, drain, then tip into the cream with the grated Parmesan. Blitz with an electric hand blender until smooth.

3 Cook the pasta according to the packet instructions, then throw in the asparagus tips 2 minutes before the end of the cooking time. Gently reheat the cream, drain the pasta, then tip into a bowl with the cream. Toss, divide between two pasta bowls, top with Parmesan shavings and serve.

PER SERVING 913 kcals, protein 28g, carbs 100g, fat 47g, sat fat 26g, fibre 5g, sugar 5g, salt 0.53g

Tuna arrabiata pasta gratin

Swap the usual creamy tuna bake for this low-fat, full-on taste alternative. Wholemeal pasta can take longer to boil than white, so check it's cooked to your liking.

TAKES 30 MINUTES • SERVES 4

1 tsp olive oil
1 red and 1 yellow pepper, deseeded and sliced
2 garlic cloves, crushed
pinch of crushed dried chillies
2 × 400g cans chopped tomatoes
50g/2oz pitted mixed olives, whole or roughly chopped (optional)
pinch of caster sugar
250g/9oz wholemeal pasta shapes
2 × 200g cans tuna steak in spring water, drained and flaked
25g/1oz fresh wholemeal breadcrumbs
2 tbsp grated Parmesan
green salad, to serve (optional)

1 Heat the oil in a large pan and fry the peppers for about 5 minutes until starting to caramelise. Add the garlic and chillies, cook for 30 seconds, then tip in the tomatoes and olives (if using). Season, add the sugar, bring to the boil, then simmer, uncovered, for 10 minutes.
2 Meanwhile, cook the pasta according to the packet instructions. Drain the pasta and heat the grill to high. Mix the pasta into the tomato sauce, along with the tuna and tip into a large ovenproof dish. Combine the breadcrumbs and Parmesan, and scatter over the top. Grill for 3–4 minutes until the topping is crisp and golden. Serve with a green salad, if you like.

PER SERVING 365 kcals, protein 30g, carbs 54g, fat 5g, sat fat 1g, fibre 9g, sugar 11g, salt 0.75g

Tomato & basil pasta sauce

Make this great-value sauce in double quantities and freeze. Perfect for pasta, meat and fish, it's easy to adapt – for example, add chilli and fried bacon for an arrabiata.

TAKES ABOUT 5 MINUTES • SERVES 4 (MAKES 350ML/12FL OZ)

1 tbsp olive oil
1 garlic clove, crushed
400g can chopped tomatoes
1 tsp vegetable stock powder or
   ½ crumbled stock cube
1 tbsp tomato purée
1 tsp sugar
a few basil leaves

1 Heat the oil in a pan, add the garlic, then gently fry for 1 minute. Tip in all the other ingredients, except the basil, then bring to the boil. Reduce the heat, then simmer, uncovered, for 5 minutes, stirring occasionally.

2 To finish, tear the basil leaves and stir them into the sauce.

PER SERVING 52 kcals, protein 2g, carbs 5g, fat 3g, sat fat 1g, fibre 1g, sugar 4g, salt 0.28g

Fusilli with glorious green spinach sauce

Add colour to your day with a plateful of this vibrant pasta with its easy no-cook spinach sauce.

TAKES 20 MINUTES • SERVES 4

400g/14oz fusilli pasta spirals
200g/8oz bag baby leaf spinach
1 garlic clove
250g tub mascarpone
juice of ½ large lemon
25g/1oz grated Parmesan, plus extra
    to sprinkle (optional)
50g/2oz ready-toasted pine nuts

1 Cook the pasta according to the packet instructions. Meanwhile, put half the spinach in a food processor with the garlic, mascarpone, lemon juice and Parmesan, then whizz until you are left with a smooth sauce.

2 Drain the pasta thoroughly and return to the pan over a low heat. Stir in the sauce, pine nuts and remaining spinach, until the spinach has just wilted. Season and serve with extra Parmesan sprinkled over, if you like.

PER SERVING 770 kcals, protein 20g, carbs 80g, fat 43g, sat fat 21g, fibre 5g, sugar 7g, salt 0.53g

Goat's cheese & garlic linguine with crisp pancetta

Fuss free but full of flavour, you'll be making this pasta dish again and again. Thin-cut streaky bacon makes a good alternative to pancetta if need be.

TAKES 35 MINUTES • SERVES 4

1 garlic bulb, broken into cloves, unpeeled
4 tbsp extra-virgin olive oil, plus extra for drizzling
3 onions, finely sliced
2 tbsp fresh thyme leaves
12 slices pancetta
400g/14oz linguine
200g/8oz firm goat's cheese
handful of chopped flat-leaf parsley, to garnish

1 Heat oven to 200C/180C fan/gas 6. Loosely wrap the garlic cloves in some foil with 1 teaspoon of the oil. Put in a roasting tin and cook for 20 minutes until soft. Meanwhile, heat 2 tablespoons of the oil and fry the onions for 15 minutes until caramelised, adding the thyme for the final 5 minutes.

2 In a separate pan, dry-fry the pancetta until golden and crisp. Cook the pasta according to the packet instructions.

3 Pop the roasted garlic cloves out of their skins, add to the onions, then stir in the remaining oil. Drain the pasta, then toss through the onions, adding a good splash of cooking water. Crumble over the cheese and lightly stir. Season, then pile on to plates. Scatter with parsley, drizzle with some more oil and top with pancetta slices.

PER SERVING 740 kcals, protein 31g, carbs 83g, fat 34g, sat fat 13g, fibre 4g, sugar 9g, salt 2.23g

Pasta with garlicky greens

Don't just relegate greens to side-veg status; here, spinach or kale, those good-for-you winter greens, star in their own delicious pasta dish.

TAKES 40 MINUTES ● **SERVES 4**

1 tbsp olive oil

3 leeks, finely sliced

2 garlic cloves, finely chopped

250g/9oz baby leaf spinach or shredded kale

200ml/7fl oz crème fraîche

400g/14oz orecchiette or other short pasta

50g/2oz blue cheese, crumbled, to garnish

1 Heat the oil in a frying pan. Add the leeks and garlic, and let them soften for 15 minutes. Stir in the spinach or kale for a final few minutes to wilt. Kale will take a little longer than spinach. Add the crème fraîche, stir, and remove from the heat.

2 Cook the pasta according to the packet instructions. Drain the pasta, put it back in its pan, then stir in the leek sauce. Serve in bowls topped with crumbled blue cheese.

PER SERVING 644 kcals, protein 19g, carbs 80g, fat 30g, sat fat 16g, fibre 7g, sugar 6g, salt 0.52g

Pasta with mozzarella, mint & fresh tomato sauce

When the sun is shining, try tossing pasta with a fresh, light, no-cook sauce.

TAKES 30 MINUTES • SERVES 4

zest and juice of 1 lemon
1 red onion, very finely chopped
400g/14oz spaghetti
6 tbsp extra-virgin olive oil, plus extra
    for drizzling
4 tsp small capers
1 red chilli, deseeded and finely
    chopped
pinch of sugar
500g/1lb 4oz ripe cherry tomatoes,
    quartered
bunch of mint, leaves torn
handful of chives, snipped
1–2 × 125g balls buffalo mozzarella
    (depending on how lavish you feel)

1 Put the lemon zest and juice into a large bowl, tip in the onion, then season with salt and black pepper. Set aside for 10 minutes to let the onion soften a little.
2 Cook the spaghetti for 10 minutes or according to the packet instructions. Mix the oil, capers, chilli and sugar into the lemony onions, then season generously.
3 When the pasta is ready, drain, toss with a splash of oil, then let it cool. Put the pasta into the bowl with the lemony onion dressing, tip in the tomatoes and most of the herbs, then toss well. Tear in the mozzarella and toss gently. Divide among four bowls, top with the remaining herbs and drizzle with more oil to serve.

PER SERVING (with 2 mozzarella balls) 763 kcals, protein 25g, carbs 81g, fat 40g, sat fat 12g, fibre 5g, sugar 9g, salt 0.91g

Cauliflower cheese & spinach pasta bakes

Somewhere between macaroni and cauliflower cheese, these pasta bakes are perfect for a cold day.

TAKES ABOUT 1 HOUR • SERVES 6

850ml/1½ pints milk
50g/2oz plain flour
50g/2oz butter, plus extra 1 tbsp
1 tsp Dijon mustard
100g/4oz extra-mature Cheddar, grated
50g/2oz blue cheese
½ tsp finely grated nutmeg
250g/9oz penne
1kg/2lb 4oz cauliflower (2 medium),
    cut into florets
1 garlic clove, left whole
750g/1lb 10oz frozen spinach (whole
    leaf), defrosted and squeezed dry
25g/1oz toasted pine nuts

FOR THE TOMATO SAUCE

3 garlic cloves, sliced
2 tbsp extra-virgin olive oil
700g jar tomato passata

1 For the tomato sauce, soften the sliced garlic in the oil, then add the passata. Season and simmer for 20 minutes.
2 Put the milk, flour and butter into a pan. Heat, whisking non-stop, until thickened. Cool for 5 minutes then add the mustard, most of the Cheddar, half the blue cheese and half the nutmeg.
3 Boil the penne and cauliflower together for 8 minutes. Reserve a little water, then drain. Melt the extra butter in a pan and add the whole garlic clove, spinach, remaining nutmeg and seasoning. Stir for 2 minutes, then remove the garlic.
4 Heat oven to 200C/180C fan/gas 6. Set aside 300ml cheese sauce and mix the rest into the pasta. Divide half the tomato sauce among six dishes and top with some spinach. Fill with pasta mix, then cover with more spinach and tomato sauce. Top with cheese sauce, the remaining cheeses and the pine nuts. Bake for 18–20 minutes, till golden.

PER SERVING 591 kcals, protein 28g, carbs 60g, fat 29g, sat fat 13g, fibre 8g, sugar 18g, salt 1.91g

Venetian-style pasta

This recipe is ideal if you fancy something completely different to a tomatoey or creamy pasta sauce.

TAKES ABOUT 15 MINUTES
- **SERVES 2**

2 red onions, sliced
1 tbsp olive oil
200g/8oz pasta shapes
4 tsp balsamic vinegar
2 tbsp sultanas
4 tsp capers, drained and rinsed well
2 tbsp toasted pine nuts
140g/5oz spinach leaves

1 Start frying the onions in the oil in a non-stick frying pan – you'll need to cook them for about 10 minutes until they're very soft. Meanwhile, cook the pasta according to the packet instructions.

2 Stir the vinegar, sultanas, capers and most of the pine nuts into the soft onions with some seasoning, then cook for 1 minute more to soften the sultanas. Stir in the spinach with a splash of pasta water. Drain the pasta, then toss with the onion mix – the spinach should wilt as you do so. Divide between two bowls, scatter with the remaining pine nuts and serve.

PER SERVING 568 kcals, protein 17g, carbs 97g, fat 15g, sat fat 2g, fibre 7g, sugar 21g, salt 0.74g

Creamy ham, leek & mushroom spaghetti

Creamy pasta needn't be off the menu when you're watching your weight – this one's delicious and low in fat.

TAKES 30 MINUTES • SERVES 4

2 tsp olive oil
2 medium leeks, thinly sliced
200g/8oz chestnut mushrooms, sliced
2 garlic cloves, crushed
300g/10oz spaghetti
140g/5oz low-fat soft cheese
85g/3oz wafer-thin smoked ham,
   shredded
small pack of basil
25g/1oz grated Parmesan

1 Heat the oil in a large pan, stir in the leeks, 2 tablespoons water and some seasoning, cover, then cook for around 5 minutes over a medium heat until softened. Add the mushrooms and garlic, then cook for 3 minutes more.
2 Meanwhile, cook the spaghetti according to the packet instructions, then drain, reserving a little of the cooking water.
3 Stir the soft cheese into the leek and mushroom mixture, adding enough of the reserved pasta water to give a sauce-like consistency. Don't boil the sauce once the cheese has been added, as it might split. Add the ham, basil leaves and Parmesan, then toss in the spaghetti.

PER SERVING 384 kcals, protein 21g, carbs 53g, fat 11g, sat fat 5g, fibre 8g, sugar 6g, salt 1.38g

Bows with tuna, olives & capers

If you like a good tuna niçoise, you'll love this pasta with salty olives, capers and tuna.
For a real treat, try tuna packed in olive oil, and use some of that oil for the sauce.

TAKES 20 MINUTES • SERVES 4

400g/14oz pasta bows
6 tbsp extra-virgin olive oil
2 garlic cloves, crushed
2 × 200g cans tuna, drained
85g/3oz pitted black olives, halved
2 tbsp capers, rinsed
small bunch of flat-leaf parsley, roughly
   chopped

1 Cook the pasta according to the packet instructions then drain, reserving a few tablespoons of water in the bottom of the pan.
2 Return the pasta to the pan over a low heat, stir in the oil and garlic, and allow to infuse for 1 minute. Toss through the remaining ingredients, season, and serve straight away.

PER SERVING 677 kcals, protein 35g, carbs 76g, fat 28g, sat fat 4g, fibre 4g, sugar 2g, salt 2.36g

Pumpkin pasta with goat's cheese & sage butter

An autumnal dish that will bring colour and flavour to the table. You can also try making this with gnocchi instead of pasta.

TAKES 45 MINUTES • SERVES 4

800g/1lb 12oz pumpkin, peeled, deseeded and cut into 2cm/¾in cubes

2 tbsp olive oil

300g/10oz garganelli or penne

85g/3oz butter

4 tbsp chopped sage, plus extra leaves left whole, to garnish

25g/1oz pine nuts

175g/6oz crumbly goat's cheese, such as Capricorn

1 Heat oven to 200C/fan 180C/gas 6. Place the pumpkin on a baking sheet, toss with the oil and season well. Roast for 30 minutes until tender.

2 Meanwhile, cook the pasta according to the packet instructions until just tender. Drain, reserving a little of the cooking water, then return to the pan with enough water to stop it drying out.

3 When the pumpkin is cooked, stir it into the pasta. Heat the butter in a frying pan and add the chopped sage, pine nuts and whole sage leaves. Cook over a medium heat until the butter and nuts start to brown and the sage crisps. Lift out and retain the whole leaves, then toss the pasta into the butter and crumble over the cheese. Toss until the cheese begins to melt. Serve in bowls, topped with the whole sage leaves.

PER SERVING 683 kcals, protein 19g, carbs 63g, fat 41g, sat fat 21g, fibre 4g, sugar 5g, salt 1.17g

Marinated figs with prosciutto, mozzarella & basil

These cute bites are a step up from the '60s favourite of cheese and pineapple on sticks. If some of your guests are vegetarian, prepare a few sticks without prosciutto.

TAKES ABOUT 15 MINUTES, PLUS MARINATING • MAKES 16

2 large or 4 small ripe figs
3 tbsp basil-infused oil
2 tsp red wine vinegar
8 slices prosciutto, halved lengthways
16 bocconcini (baby mozzarella balls)
16 medium-sized basil leaves

1 Cut the figs into 16 wedges and sit them in a non-metallic bowl. Mix together the oil and vinegar, then pour it over the figs. Season well with salt and black pepper, then leave to marinate at room temperature for about 30 minutes.
2 When the figs have marinated, thread the wedges on to 16 short wooden skewers with some prosciutto, a mozzarella ball and a basil leaf on each. The order in which you thread them is entirely up to you.
3 Once you have made all 16, sit them on a plate and drizzle over the remaining marinade. Serve at room temperature rather than straight from the fridge, so all the flavours are at their best.

PER SKEWER 61 kcals, protein 4g, carbs 1g, fat 5g, sat fat 2g, fibre none, added sugar none, salt 0.48g

Roast chicken with pancetta & ricotta stuffing balls

A classic roast chicken is made extra special with these Italian stuffing balls.

TAKES 2 HOURS 10 MINUTES ●
SERVES 4 WITH LEFTOVERS

1 whole chicken (about 1.5kg/3lb 5oz)
3 tbsp extra-virgin olive oil

FOR THE STUFFING BALLS

140g/5oz fresh bread (about 3–4 slices)
handful of flat-leaf parsley, chopped
140g/5oz ricotta
100g/4oz Parmesan, freshly grated
handful of thyme, leaves chopped
handful of basil, leaves chopped
2 garlic cloves, finely chopped
2 eggs
12 thin slices pancetta or streaky
  bacon

1 Heat oven to 180C/160C fan/gas 4. Season the chicken, then put it into a large roasting dish. Rub it all over with the oil then roast for 1½ hours, spooning the oil and juices over the bird a few times during cooking.

2 Meanwhile, make the stuffing. Whizz the bread and parsley to crumbs in a food processor. Tip in to a large bowl then mix with the rest of the ingredients, apart from the pancetta or bacon. Shape into 12 balls, then wrap a slice of pancetta or bacon around each.

3 Test to see if the chicken is done by inserting a skewer into the thigh meat; if the juices run clear remove it from the roasting dish, put it on a serving plate, loosely cover it with foil and leave it to rest. Pour away any excess fat from the dish and tip in the stuffing balls. Roast for 20 minutes until crisp and golden. Serve alongside the chicken.

PER SERVING 828 kcals, protein 71g, carbs 19g, fat 52g, sat fat 19g, fibre 1g, sugar 2g, salt 2.57g

Parmesan bake (Melanzane alla parmigiana)

*This delicious supper can be made in advance and in fact improves with age. Serve
with a crisp salad and crusty bread to mop up the juices.*

TAKES 1 HOUR • SERVES 6

2 garlic cloves, crushed
6 tbsp olive oil
2 × 400g cans chopped tomatoes
2 tbsp tomato purée
4 aubergines, cut into long 5mm/¼in-
    thick slices
85g/3oz Parmesan, freshly grated
20g pack basil, leaves torn, plus a few
    extra left whole, to garnish (optional)
1 egg, beaten

1 Heat oven to 200C/180C fan/gas 6. In
a shallow pan, mix together the garlic and
4 tablespoons of the oil. Cook over a high
heat for 3 minutes, tip in the tomatoes,
then simmer for 8 minutes, stirring every
now and then. Stir in the tomato purée.
2 Meanwhile, heat a griddle pan until
very hot. Brush a few of the aubergine
slices with a little oil, then cook over a
high heat until well browned and cooked
through, about 5–7 minutes. Turn
halfway through cooking. Lift on to
kitchen paper and do the next batch.
3 When all the aubergines are cooked,
lay a few in an ovenproof dish, then
spoon over some tomato sauce. Sprinkle
with some of the Parmesan and basil
leaves. Add seasoning, then repeat this
process. Finally, pour the egg over the
top, sprinkle over a little more Parmesan,
then bake for 20 minutes or until the
topping is golden. Garnish with a few
whole basil leaves, if you like.

PER SERVING 225 kcals, protein 10g, carbs 8g,
fat 17g, sat fat 5g, fibre 5g, sugar 7g, salt 0.52g

Roasted vegetable lasagne

You can freeze this lasagne, uncooked. Defrost overnight in the fridge, then add an extra 5 minutes cooking time or cook from frozen for 1¼ hours at 180C/160C fan/gas 4.

TAKES 1 HOUR 35 MINUTES

● **SERVES 6**

85g/3oz butter
85g/3oz plain flour
750ml/1¼ pints milk
8 tbsp olive oil, plus extra for greasing
3 red peppers, deseeded and cut into
    large chunks
2 aubergines, cut into 5mm/¼in slices
600ml/1 pint ready-made or
    homemade tomato sauce
300g pack fresh lasagne sheets
125g ball mozzarella, torn into strips
handful of cherry tomatoes, halved

1 For the white sauce, melt the butter in a pan, stir in the flour, then cook for 2 minutes. Slowly whisk in the milk then bring to the boil, stirring until the sauce is thickened and smooth. Season to taste.
2 Heat oven to 200C/180C fan/gas 6. Lightly grease two large baking sheets, then add the peppers and aubergines. Toss with the oil, season well, then roast for 25 minutes until lightly browned.
3 Reduce oven to 180C/160C fan/gas 4. Grease a large ovenproof dish, then cover the base with a third of the vegetables, then a third of the tomato sauce. Top with a layer of lasagne, then drizzle over a quarter of the white sauce. Repeat until you have three layers of pasta, finishing with a layer of pasta on top. Cover the lasagne in the remaining white sauce, scatter with the mozzarella and tomatoes, then bake for 45 minutes until bubbling and golden.

PER SERVING 461 kcals, protein 13g, carbs 37g, fat 29g, sat fat 9g, fibre 5g, sugar 14g, salt 0.59g

Rosemary & anchovy lamb steaks

Probably the cheapest way to buy the lamb is from your butcher; buy legs, then have them sliced into steaks for you. You'll need one whole leg and a half leg for 12 steaks.

TAKES 25 MINUTES, PLUS MARINATING
● **SERVES 12, EASILY HALVED**

3 lemons
6 anchovy fillets, roughly chopped
2 tbsp roughly chopped rosemary, plus
    extra sprigs, to garnish
4 tbsp olive oil
12 lamb leg steaks, about
    250–300g/9–10oz each
lemon wedges, to garnish

1 Finely grate the zest from the lemons and mix with the anchovies, rosemary and the oil in a food processor, then blend to a rough paste. Put the lamb in a large food bag or bowl, then pour over the marinade, massaging it into the meat. Marinate in the fridge for at least 1 hour, preferably overnight.

2 Heat the grill to high (or the barbecue if the weather's good), then cook the lamb for 4–5 minutes each side (depending on the thickness of the lamb and how you like it cooked) until nicely browned on the outside. Transfer to a board, cover with foil and leave to rest for 10 minutes. Serve sprinkled with rosemary sprigs and lemon wedges for squeezing over.

PER SERVING 348 kcals, protein 50g, carbs none, fat 17g, sat fat 8g, fibre none, sugar none, salt 0.37g

Pumpkin, sage & Parmesan gratin

This makes a great veggie main course served with a salad, or a delicious, substantial side dish cooked alongside a roast.

TAKES 1¼ HOURS • SERVES 4, EASILY DOUBLED

1kg/2lb 4oz pumpkin or winter squash, peeled, deseeded and chopped into large chunks
3 tbsp olive oil
2 garlic cloves, chopped
small bunch of sage, most leaves roughly chopped, some left whole
142ml pot double cream
50g/2oz Parmesan, grated

1 Heat oven to 200C/180C fan/gas 6. In a large gratin dish, toss the pumpkin with the oil, garlic and sage and season with salt and black pepper. Roast for 40 minutes until soft.

2 Remove the pumpkin from the oven and increase oven to 220C/200C fan/gas 7. Lift out and reserve the whole sage leaves. Drizzle over the cream and scatter the cheese. Return to the oven for around 20 minutes until bubbling and golden, then finish with the whole sage leaves to serve.

PER SERVING 233 kcals, protein 15g, carbs 8g, fat 16g, sat fat 7g, fibre 1g, sugar none, salt 3.9g

Olive & lemon-crusted rack of lamb with a warm salad

Great for entertaining and light enough to turn into an al-fresco dish if the weather is good. Get your butcher to French-trim the racks for you.

TAKES ABOUT 55 MINUTES ● SERVES 4, EASILY DOUBLED

FOR THE LAMB

2 × 6-bone racks new-season lamb
zest of 1 lemon, plus 1 tbsp juice
3 tbsp chopped flat-leaf parsley
1 tbsp chopped mint
85g/3oz green olives stuffed with anchovies, finely chopped
2 tbsp extra-virgin olive oil
2 tbsp pesto

FOR THE WARM SALAD

300g/10oz red-skinned potatoes, cut into chunks
100g/4oz fine green beans, trimmed
½ head radicchio, shredded
2 tbsp extra-virgin olive oil
1 garlic clove, crushed
handful of Parmesan shavings

1 Heat oven to 240C/220C fan/gas 9. Place the racks on a board, fat-side up, and trim off any excess fat. Score the remaining fat in a criss-cross pattern. Mix the lemon zest with the parsley, mint, olives and oil. Spread the pesto over the racks, then press the olive crust over the top. Put into a roasting tin and roast for 25–30 minutes for medium.

2 While the lamb is cooking, boil the potatoes in a pan of water from cold for 8 minutes until almost tender. Add the beans and cook for 4 minutes more, then drain the beans and potatoes, and cool briefly under the cold tap. Tip into a mixing bowl and toss with the remaining ingredients and the lemon juice. Rest the lamb for 5 minutes once it's ready, then slice into chops and serve with the salad.

PER SERVING 607 kcals, protein 51g, carbs 15g, fat 39g, sat fat 14g, fibre 3g, sugar 2g, salt 1.87g

Pancetta-wrapped trout

Freshwater trout is a much underused, yet sustainable and delicious British fish.
The trout can be wrapped in pancetta the day before and chilled until ready to roast.

**TAKES 30 MINUTES • SERVES 2,
EASILY DOUBLED**

1 lemon
2 small trout, rainbow or brown,
    cleaned
1 large bunch thyme
1 garlic clove, chopped
4 slices pancetta or rashers smoked
    streaky bacon
4 tbsp olive oil
100g/4oz fine green beans
2 tbsp toasted flaked almonds

1 Heat oven to 220C/200C fan/gas 7. Cut half the lemon into four thin slices and juice the other half. Score each fish three times on one side. Put the fish on a baking sheet, scored-side up, and season liberally inside and out. Stuff each fish cavity with a little thyme, a sprinkling of garlic and a lemon slice. Lay the rest of the thyme on top of the fish and top with a lemon slice.

2 Wrap the pancetta or bacon around the fish, holding the lemon and thyme in place. Drizzle with 1 tablespoon of the oil then bake for 20 minutes until the pancetta is golden and the fish is completely cooked.

3 Meanwhile, boil the beans in a pan of salted water for 4–5 minutes until just cooked and still vibrant. Drain and toss with the lemon juice, remaining oil and the almonds. Serve the fish with the beans on the side.

PER SERVING 554 kcals, protein 45g, carbs 4g, fat 40g, sat fat 7g, fibre 2g, sugar 3g, salt 1g

Seared beef with wild mushrooms & balsamic vinegar

You can't go wrong with this seared beef fillet and its delicious sauce. The dish is rich in flavour, yet still light enough to leave you with room for dessert.

TAKES 35 MINUTES, PLUS
MARINATING • SERVES 2

400g/14oz piece beef fillet
3 tbsp olive oil
leaves from 1 rosemary sprig, bruised
1 garlic clove, crushed
2 tbsp butter
200g/8oz mixed wild mushrooms
200ml/7fl oz good beef stock
1 tsp balsamic vinegar

1 Rub the beef with 1 tablespoon of the oil, the rosemary and garlic, and leave for at least 1 hour. Make sure the beef is at room temperature before cooking.
2 Heat oven to 200C/180C fan/gas 6. Heat a non-stick, ovenproof pan until very hot but not smoking. Rub most of the marinade from the beef, season well, then sear it in the pan until dark brown all over – roughly 5 minutes in total. Transfer the pan to the oven, then roast for 10 minutes for medium–rare. Leave to rest for 15 minutes.
3 Meanwhile, heat 1 tablespoon of the butter and the remaining oil in a large pan, then season and fry the mushrooms until golden. Tip into a bowl.
4 Add the stock to the mushroom pan, then reduce by two-thirds. Tip in the mushrooms, balsamic and remaining butter, and warm through. Add any resting juices, then season and serve.

PER SERVING 526 kcals, protein 46g, carbs 3g, fat 37g, sat fat 15g, fibre 1g, sugar 1g, salt 1.04g

Open ravioli with squash & porcini

Vegetarians often get a poor deal at dinner parties, but this recipe looks and tastes special – and it is easy to manage if you're also cooking a roast.

TAKES ABOUT 1 HOUR 20 MINUTES ●
SERVES 2, EASILY HALVED OR DOUBLED

FOR THE SQUASH

450g/1lb butternut squash, peeled, deseeded and chopped

25g/1oz butter

generous grating of nutmeg

25g/1oz vegetarian Parmesan cheese, coarsely grated, plus extra to garnish

FOR THE PORCINI DRESSING

1 tbsp finely chopped dried porcini mushrooms

2 tbsp olive oil

1 tsp balsamic vinegar

2 tsp soy sauce

TO SERVE

85g/3oz chestnut mushrooms, quartered

1 fat garlic clove, crushed

100g bag baby spinach

4 sheets fresh lasagne, halved

generous pinch of saffron

shavings of Parmesan

1 Put the squash and butter in a pan with 5 tablespoons water. Tightly cover then cook for 15 minutes until just tender. Roughly mash with seasoning, nutmeg and Parmesan. Set aside.

2 For the dressing, put the porcini in a bowl with 3 tablespoons boiling water. Cover and cook for 1 minute in the microwave, then set aside to cool. Mix 1 tablespoon of oil, the vinegar and soy sauce, then add the soaked mushrooms and liquid, straining out any grit.

3 Boil a large pan of salted water. Meanwhile, fry the chestnut mushrooms in the remaining oil. Add the garlic and cook briefly. Pierce the bag of spinach and wilt it in the microwave for 1 minute. Reheat the squash too.

4 Boil the lasagne with the saffron for 1 minute until just tender, then drain. Stack the spinach, pasta and squash on two plates, scatter round the garlicky mushrooms, then finish with Parmesan.

PER SERVING 504 kcals, protein 17g, carbs 49g, fat 28g, sat fat 11g, fibre 7g, sugar 13g, salt 1.61g

Sage & prosciutto pork with rich mushroom ragout

Cooking fillets of pork in prosciutto parcels not only protects them from drying out in the oven but also adds a delicious savouriness.

TAKES ABOUT 1½ HOURS ● SERVES 6

3 pork tenderloins, about 300g/10oz each
18 slices prosciutto
18 sage leaves
juice of 1 lemon
1 tbsp roughly chopped flat-leaf parsley, to garnish

FOR THE SAUCE

3 shallots, finely chopped
2 tbsp olive oil
25g/1oz dried porcini mushrooms, soaked in 300ml/½ pint water for 20 minutes, soaking liquid reserved
250g/9oz chestnut mushrooms, sliced
4 tbsp Marsala or dry sherry
1 tbsp tomato purée

1 Heat oven to 190C/170C fan/gas 5. Halve each piece of pork to make six smaller tenderloins, then split each one almost in half along the length. Open out and bat flat with a rolling pin. Overlap three slices of prosciutto on a board and put one pork tenderloin and three sage leaves on top. Season and sprinkle with lemon juice. Roll up, then tie with string. Repeat with each piece of meat. Roast the pork for 25–30 minutes.

2 Gently fry the shallots in the oil for 5 minutes. Drain the porcini mushrooms, reserving the liquid, chop, then add to the pan with the fresh mushrooms. Season and cook until softened.

3 Splash in the Marsala or sherry, and reduce. Add the mushroom soaking liquid, tomato purée and seasoning. Bubble for 2 minutes. Serve with the pork and a garnish of parsley.

PER SERVING 357 kcals, protein 43g, carbs 4g, fat 18g, sat fat 5g, fibre 1g, added sugar none, salt 1.77g

Pizza margherita

One of the best things about making pizza is choosing the toppings; vary this basic recipe with ham, salami, mushrooms, goat's cheese – whatever takes your fancy.

TAKES ABOUT 35 MINUTES • SERVES 4 (MAKES 2 PIZZAS)

FOR THE BASE

300g/10oz strong bread flour, plus extra for dusting
1 tsp fast-action yeast (from a sachet or tub)
1 tsp salt
1 tbsp olive oil, plus extra for drizzling

FOR THE TOMATO SAUCE

100g/4oz passata
handful of fresh basil leaves or 1 tsp dried
1 garlic clove, crushed

FOR THE TOPPING

125g ball mozzarella, sliced
handful of grated or shaved Parmesan
handful of cherry tomatoes, halved
handful of basil leaves

1 Put the flour, yeast and salt in a large bowl; stir. Pour in 200ml/7fl oz warm water and the oil, and mix to a soft, fairly wet dough. Knead on a floured surface for 5 minutes until smooth. Cover with a tea towel. Leave the dough to rise, if you like, but it's not essential for a thin crust.

2 Mix together the sauce ingredients. Split the dough in two. On a floured surface, roll the dough into large, thin rounds, about 25cm wide. Lift the rounds on to two floured baking sheets.

3 Heat oven to 240C/220C fan/gas 9. Put another baking sheet on the top shelf of the oven. Smooth the sauce over the pizza bases then top with cheeses, tomatoes, a little more oil and some seasoning. Put one pizza, still on its baking sheet, on top of the preheated sheet. Bake for 8–10 minutes until crisp. Serve with a little more oil and scatter over the basil leaves. Repeat with the other pizza.

PER SERVING 431 kcals, protein 19g, carbs 59g, fat 15g, sat fat 7g, fibre 3g, sugar 2g, salt 1.87g

Mushroom-stuffed chicken with lemon thyme risotto

This porcini stuffing has a really robust flavour that would also be wonderful in a whole roast chicken.

TAKES ABOUT 2 HOURS ● SERVES 4

FOR THE CHICKEN AND STUFFING

25g/1oz dried porcini mushrooms, soaked in 250ml/9fl oz water for 30 minutes, soaking liquid reserved

1 onion, finely chopped

1 tbsp olive oil

150g pack baby button mushrooms, finely chopped

2 thyme sprigs or lemon thyme sprigs, leaves removed and chopped

175ml/6fl oz white wine

4 chicken breasts, skin on

FOR THE LEMON THYME RISOTTO

1 tbsp butter

1 tbsp olive oil

2 celery sticks, finely chopped

1 small onion, finely chopped

140g/5oz risotto rice

600ml/1 pint hot chicken stock

2 thyme sprigs or lemon thyme sprigs, leaves removed and chopped

juice and zest of ½ lemon

50g/2oz Parmesan, grated

1 Heat oven to 180C/160C fan/gas 4. Finely chop the porcini. Soften the onion in the oil for 5 minutes. Add the porcini, button mushrooms and thyme, season, then turn up the heat, for 5 minutes.

2 Add the wine, reduce until nearly dry, then add 50ml/2fl oz porcini liquid and reduce until syrupy. Cool for 2 minutes, then spoon under the skin of the chicken breasts. Season, then roast for around 20 minutes, until cooked and golden.

3 For the risotto, heat the butter and oil in a pan, add the celery and onion, then cook for 5 minutes. Add the rice, stir, then cook for 1 minute. Gradually add the stock, a ladleful at a time, stirring with each addition until absorbed. Continue until oozing and thick – about 20 minutes. Stir in the thyme, lemon juice and zest and Parmesan.

4 Serve topped with the chicken, some extra Parmesan and any pan juices.

PER SERVING 501 kcals, protein 47g, carbs 36g, fat 18g, sat fat 6g, fibre 3g, sugar 6g, salt 1.67g

Italian-style beef stew

Beef stew normally takes hours, but not with this clever recipe, made with already-tender frying steak. Perfect with the creamy polenta on page 166.

TAKES 40 MINUTES • SERVES 4, EASILY DOUBLED

1 onion, sliced
1 garlic clove, sliced
2 tbsp olive oil
300g/10oz thinly sliced beef steak
1 yellow pepper, deseeded and thinly
   sliced
400g can chopped tomatoes
1 sprig rosemary, chopped
handful of pitted olives
mash or polenta, to serve

1 In a large pan, cook the onion and garlic in the oil for 5 minutes until softened and turning golden. Tip in the beef, pepper, tomatoes and rosemary, then bring to the boil.

2 Simmer for 15 minutes until the meat is cooked through, adding some boiling water if needed. Stir through the olives and serve with mash or polenta.

PER SERVING 225 kcals, protein 25g, carbs 7g, fat 11g, sat fat 3g, fibre 2g, sugar 6g, salt 0.87g

Roast chicken with olive salsa

A tangy, spicy salsa lifts simple roast chicken legs to new levels. Serve this economical main with mashed potatoes, or one of the tasty sides starting on page 156.

TAKES 1¼ HOURS ● SERVES 6

6 whole chicken legs or 12 thighs, or a mixture of both, skin on
8 unpeeled garlic cloves
5 tbsp olive oil
few bay leaves, plus extra to garnish (optional)
200g/8oz large pitted green olives
2 small bunches flat-leaf parsley, finely chopped
2 red chillies, deseeded and finely chopped
zest of 2 oranges, juice of 1½
juice of ½ lemon

1 Heat oven to 180C/160C fan/gas 4. Mix the chicken and garlic with 1 tablespoon of the oil in a shallow roasting tin, then poke around a few bay leaves. Sprinkle with ½ teaspoon each sea salt and black pepper then roast for 30 minutes. After 30 minutes, fish out the garlic, increase the oven temperature to 220C/200C fan/gas 7 and roast for 15–20 minutes more until the chicken is golden, crispy and cooked through.

2 While the chicken is cooking, roughly chop the olives in a food processor, then scrape into a serving bowl. Stir in the parsley, chillies, orange zest and juice, lemon juice, remaining oil and some seasoning. Serve the chicken on a platter with the salsa spooned over and garnished with a few bay leaves, if you like.

PER SERVING 310 kcals, protein 17g, carbs 2g, fat 26g, sat fat 6g, fibre 1g, sugar 2g, salt 2.1g

Truffled parsnip & Parmesan bruschetta

Scented truffle oil and Parmesan make a real star of humble parsnips. Prepare the parsnip purée ahead of time so that prep is kept to a minimum.

TAKES 35 MINUTES • MAKES 12, EASILY DOUBLED

1 mini ciabatta or panini roll, cut into 12 × 0.5cm/¼in slices
1 garlic clove, halved
50g/2oz butter
3 large parsnips, halved, quartered, cored and cut into 1cm/½in cubes
1 tsp truffle oil, plus extra to drizzle (optional)
2 tbsp olive oil, plus extra to drizzle
handful of rocket leaves and 50g/2oz Parmesan shavings, to garnish

1 Heat a griddle pan and toast the bread for about 2 minutes on each side until golden and marked. Rub the cut-side of the garlic clove over each piece.

2 Heat the butter in a large frying pan, add the parsnips, season with sea salt and black pepper, then cook over a medium heat for about 20 minutes, shaking regularly until golden and softened. Add a splash of water if you need to. Remove from the heat and whizz to a purée in a food processor with both of the oils. Season to taste. Set aside at room temperature if serving on the day. Can now be chilled up to 2 days ahead.

3 To serve, top the toasts with the truffled parsnip mix (it should be at room temperature), scatter with rocket leaves and Parmesan shavings, then drizzle with a little olive oil or the truffle oil, if you like.

PER SERVING 112 kcals, protein 3g, carbs 9g, fat 8g, sat fat 3g, fibre 2g, sugar 2g, salt 0.28g

Creamy beetroot risotto

This vivid risotto is simply baked in the oven along with the beetroot, so there's no need to spend lots of time stirring at the stove.

TAKES 1 HOUR 10 MINUTES
- **SERVES 4**

500g/1lb 2oz fresh beetroot, peeled and trimmed
2 tbsp olive oil
knob of butter
1 onion, finely chopped
1 garlic clove, finely chopped
250g/9oz risotto rice
150ml/¼ pint white wine
700ml/1¼ pints hot vegetable stock
handful of grated Parmesan
4 tbsp soured cream and handful of chopped dill, to garnish

1 Heat oven to 180C/160C fan/gas 4. Cut the beets into large wedges and put them on a large sheet of foil on a baking sheet. Toss with half the oil, season, then cook for 1 hour until the beets are soft.

2 Meanwhile, heat the remaining oil with the butter in an ovenproof pan. Tip in the onion and garlic, then cook for around 3–5 minutes until translucent. Stir in the rice then add the white wine and let it bubble away for 5 minutes.

3 Stir well, then add the stock. Stir again, cover, and put in the oven. Cook for 15 minutes until the rice is soft. Remove the beetroots from the oven. Whizz a quarter of them in a food processor to make a purée, then chop the remainder into small pieces. Stir most of the Parmesan, the beetroot purée and chopped beetroot through the risotto, season, then serve topped with soured cream, dill and the remaining Parmesan.

PER SERVING 434 kcals, protein 12g, carbs 65g, fat 14g, sat fat 6g, fibre 5g, sugar 14g, salt 0.7g

Wild mushroom tartlets

The mushrooms in this recipe are completely interchangeable, so use a mix or just one sort – it's entirely up to you. Serve the tarts as an autumnal starter.

TAKES 30 MINUTES • SERVES 4

375g pack all-butter puff pastry
flour, for dusting
25g/1oz butter
300g/10oz mixed wild mushrooms or
    just one type, cleaned and sliced
25g/1oz Parmesan, finely grated
small handful of flat-leaf parsley leaves,
    chopped
1 garlic clove, finely chopped
1 egg, beaten

1 Roll out the pastry on a floured surface and cut out four circles, each about 15cm wide. Leave to chill on a lined baking sheet in the fridge.
2 Heat oven to 200C/180C fan/gas 6. Heat a large frying pan until hot, then add the butter and fry the mushrooms for 5 minutes until there is no liquid left in the pan. Season, then take off the heat and mix the mushrooms with the Parmesan, parsley and garlic.
3 Score a 1cm border around the edge of each tart, then spoon the mushrooms into the centre circle. Brush the edges with beaten egg, then bake the tarts for 20 minutes until puffed up and golden. Serve immediately.

PER SERVING 473 kcals, protein 12g, carbs 39g, fat 31g, sat fat 14g, fibre 1g, sugar 2g, salt 1.32g

Pancetta chicken wraps

If you're cooking outside you can make this in a pan on top of the barbecue, too.
Turn the chicken regularly to ensure it's cooked evenly.

TAKES 40 MINUTES • SERVES 4

200g pack smoked pancetta slices or
   thin-cut rashers streaky bacon
4 boneless skinless chicken breasts
12 fresh sage leaves
1 tbsp olive oil
4 small stems tomatoes on the vine

1 Put a quarter of the pancetta slices or bacon rashers on to a board, overlapping them slightly along their long edge. Put a chicken breast across one end, top with three sage leaves and season. Wrap the chicken in the pancetta so that it is completely enclosed. Repeat.

2 Heat oven to 200C/180C fan/gas 6. Heat the oil in a large frying pan or heavy roasting tin, then add the parcels, seam-side down. Wait until the pancetta or bacon has sealed itself, then turn a few times until the pancetta has started to turn golden. Roast for 15 minutes until golden and crisp and the chicken is cooked through.

3 Remove the parcels from the pan and leave to rest on a plate for 5 minutes. Meanwhile, add the tomatoes to the pan, shake to coat in the cooking juices, then roast for 5 minutes until the skins start to split. Serve with the chicken.

PER SERVING 339 kcals, protein 44g, carbs 1g, fat 17g, sat fat 6g, fibre 1g, sugar none, salt 2.76g

Chicken & pumpkin

Prepare this delicious chicken and pumpkin dish the day before and just pop it in the oven as your guests arrive.

TAKES 1½ HOURS • SERVES 4

20g pack dried porcini mushrooms
1 free-range chicken, about 1.5kg/3lb 5oz, jointed into 8 (or use bone-in thighs)
1 lemon, halved
2 tbsp olive oil
25g/1oz unsalted butter
1 small onion, finely chopped
300g/10oz pumpkin, peeled, deseeded and cut into 2cm/¾in cubes
200g/8oz chestnut mushrooms, roughly chopped
284ml pot double cream

1 Heat oven to 180C/160C fan/gas 4. Soak the porcini in 300ml/½ pint hot water for 30 minutes. Skin the chicken pieces then rub with the cut lemon. Heat the oil in a large ovenproof pan, then brown the chicken well. Set aside.
2 Melt the butter in a medium pan. When it stops foaming, add the onion and 1 teaspoon salt, then sauté until pale gold. Meanwhile, lift the porcini from their soaking liquid and rinse well. Pat dry and chop finely.
3 Add the porcini and pumpkin pieces to the pan with the onion and sauté for 5 minutes. Add the chestnut mushrooms then cook for 5 minutes more, stirring. Stir in the cream, 4–5 tablespoons of the porcini liquid and season. Simmer, uncovered, for 10–12 minutes until reduced slightly, then pour the sauce over the chicken. Cover, then cook in the oven for 30–40 minutes, turning the chicken once or twice, until tender.

PER SERVING 666 kcals, protein 48g, carbs 8g, fat 49g, sat fat 27g, fibre 2g, sugar none, salt 1.72g

Slow-roast tomatoes with cured ham & artichokes

Semi-dried tomatoes are easy to find, but there's nothing like slow-roasting your own. The salt helps them dry out in the oven, but you don't taste it in the finished result.

TAKES ABOUT 3½ HOURS • SERVES 4 AS A STARTER, EASILY DOUBLED
100g/4oz sea salt flakes
4–6 plum tomatoes, halved
8 slices prosciutto or other cured ham
1 × jar griddled artichokes
handful of black olives
handful of flat-leaf parsley
extra-virgin olive oil, to garnish
breadsticks, to serve

1 Heat oven to 140C/120C fan/gas 1. Make a thick layer of salt on a baking sheet, top with the tomatoes, cut-side up, then slowly roast for 3 hours until they are semi dried. Remove from the salt and, if keeping for longer than a day, store in a sterilised jar completely submerged in olive oil.
2 To serve, arrange two slices of prosciutto or ham on each serving plate. Toss the tomatoes, artichokes, olives and parsley in a little oil, then arrange in the centre. Serve with breadsticks.

PER SERVING 185 kcals, protein 6g, carbs 5g, fat 16g, sat fat 3g, fibre 3g, sugar 4g, salt 3g

Zingy courgettes & spinach

Half salad, half side veg, this is a wonderful way to use up summer courgettes, and goes well with pasta and grilled meat. It also counts as one of your 5-a-day.

TAKES 10 MINUTES ● SERVES 4

1 tbsp olive oil, plus extra for drizzling
4 courgettes, cut into discs on the
    diagonal, then sliced into sticks
1 red chilli, deseeded and finely
    chopped
100g bag baby leaf spinach
zest of 1 lemon

1 Heat the oil in a frying pan. Fry the courgettes over a high heat until just tender, about 4 minutes, adding the chilli for the final minute. Take off the heat and toss though the spinach until just wilted.

2 Add the lemon zest and season to taste. Put in a serving dish and drizzle over a little more oil just before serving.

PER SERVING 78 kcals, protein 3g, carbs 3g, fat 6g, sat fat 1g, fibre 2g, sugar 3g, salt 0.09g

Focaccia with pesto & mozzarella

This focaccia really comes into its own when served with roast chicken – and it is easier to make than you'd think.

TAKES 1 HOUR, PLUS RISING
- **SERVES 4–6**

500g/1lb 2oz strong white bread flour, plus extra for dusting
1½ tsp salt
7g sachet fast-action dried yeast
2 tbsp extra-virgin olive oil, plus extra for greasing and drizzling
125g ball mozzarella, drained
5 tbsp pesto (shop-bought or homemade)
sea salt, to sprinkle (optional)

1 Put the flour, salt and yeast into a large bowl and mix together. Tip in the oil and 325ml/11fl oz warm water, then mix well and bring together in a ball of dough.

2 Knead on a lightly floured surface for 10 minutes until smooth and bouncy, then put the dough in a well-oiled bowl and cover with a little more oil and a tea towel or cling film. Leave in a warm spot for 1 hour until doubled in size.

3 Press the dough out over a baking sheet until it's about 20x30cm in size. Loosely cover with a tea towel then leave to rise again for 30–40 minutes or until it is about 50 per cent bigger than before.

4 Heat oven to 180C/160C fan/gas 4. Poke dimples in the dough then bake for 15 minutes. Tear the mozzarella over then bake for another 5–10 minutes until golden and risen. Drizzle over the pesto and scatter with a little sea salt, if you like, to serve.

PER SERVING (4) 638 kcals, protein 25g, carbs 96g, fat 20g, sat fat 6g, fibre 4g, sugar 2g, salt 2.42g

Crispy new potato bake

Punctuated with capers, olives and rosemary, these potatoes go perfectly with simply cooked fish.

TAKES 1 HOUR 10 MINUTES

● **SERVES 4**

1kg/2lb 4oz Jersey Royal or small new potatoes

handful of small capers

2 handfuls of pitted black olives

1 tbsp thyme leaves

small bunch of rosemary, broken into sprigs

6 tbsp extra-virgin olive oil

1 tbsp white wine vinegar

1 Heat oven to 240C/220C fan/gas 9. Boil the potatoes for about 12 minutes until they are quite soft. Drain, slice in half, then tip into a bowl. Tip the capers, olives and herbs on top of the potatoes, then add most of the oil and a little seasoning. Stir together, lightly crushing the potatoes.

2 Line a medium Swiss roll-type tin with baking parchment, leaving some hanging over the sides. Tip the potatoes into the tin and flatten down. Mix together the vinegar and remaining oil, drizzle over the potatoes, then bake for 40 minutes until golden.

PER SERVING 355 kcals, protein 5g, carbs 41g, fat 20g, sat fat 3g, fibre 4g, sugar 3g, salt 0.9g

Garlic bread toasts

Mop up your favourite pasta sauce with a slice of this moreish garlic bread.

TAKES 15 MINUTES ● SERVES 12, EASILY HALVED

140g/5oz butter, softened
4–6 garlic cloves, crushed
handful of parsley, chopped
2 ciabatta loaves
2 tbsp finely grated Parmesan

1 Heat the grill to medium–high. Mix together the butter, garlic and parsley in a bowl. Slice the breads in half along their length and put on to a baking sheet. Toast the crust side for 2 minutes until really crisp.

2 Turn the bread over and spread the garlic butter on the untoasted cut sides, then sprinkle with the Parmesan. Grill for 5 minutes or until toasty and golden. Let cool for 1 minute before cutting into thick slices.

PER SERVING 230 kcals, protein 6g, carbs 26g, fat 12g, sat fat 7g, fibre 1g, sugar 2g, salt 0.89g

Squash & barley salad with balsamic vinaigrette

You could almost imagine this vibrant salad piled high in a smart deli – yet all of the ingredients are straight from the supermarket. Brilliant!

TAKES 30 MINUTES, PLUS COOLING

- **SERVES 8**

1 butternut squash, peeled, deseeded and cut into long pieces

1 tbsp olive oil

250g/9oz pearl barley

300g/10oz Tenderstem broccoli, cut into medium-sized pieces

100g/4oz sun-blushed tomatoes, sliced

1 small red onion, diced

2 tbsp pumpkin seeds

1 tbsp small capers, rinsed

15 black olives, pitted

20g pack basil, leaves chopped

FOR THE DRESSING

5 tbsp balsamic vinegar

6 tbsp extra-virgin olive oil

1 tbsp Dijon mustard

1 garlic clove, finely chopped

1 Heat oven to 200C/180C fan/gas 6. Put the squash on a baking sheet and toss with the oil. Roast for 20 minutes. Meanwhile, boil the barley for about 25 minutes in a pan of salted water until tender, but al dente.

2 While both are cooking, whisk the dressing ingredients in a small bowl, then season with salt and black pepper. Drain the barley, then tip it into a bowl and pour over the dressing. Mix well and let it cool.

3 Boil the broccoli in a pan of salted water until just tender, then drain and rinse in cold water. Drain and pat dry. Add the broccoli and remaining ingredients to the barley, and mix well. This will keep for 3 days in the fridge and is delicious warm or cold.

PER SERVING 301 kcals, protein 6g, carbs 40g, fat 14g, sat fat 2g, fibre 4g, sugar 9g, salt 0.55g

Creamy polenta with spinach

Polenta is far from bland once there's mascarpone and spinach stirred through.
Add a little grated Parmesan too, if you like.

TAKES 5 MINUTES ● SERVES 4

175g/6oz quick-cook polenta
5 tbsp mascarpone
100g bag spinach leaves

1 Cook the polenta according to the packet instructions.
2 When the polenta is softened and smooth, stir through the mascarpone and spinach. Leave for 30 seconds until the spinach has just begun to wilt, stir again, then serve.

PER SERVING 240 kcals, protein 5g, carbs 33g, fat 10g, sat fat 6g, fibre 2g, added sugar none, salt 0.14g

Italian bean salad

Help yourself to plenty of this salad – it's good for you, as well as being a totally delicious and hassle-free dish.

TAKES 5 MINUTES • SERVES 8, EASILY HALVED

1 bunch spring onions
2 garlic cloves, crushed
1 red chilli, deseeded and finely chopped
2 × 400g cans cannellini beans, drained and rinsed
200g can butter beans, drained and rinsed
6 tbsp olive oil
2 tbsp white wine vinegar
handful of flat-leaf parsley leaves, finely chopped

1 Finely chop the spring onions and put into a bowl with the garlic and chilli.
2 Mix in the cannellini and butter beans. Whisk the oil with the vinegar and plenty of seasoning. Stir through the salad with plenty of parsley.

PER SERVING 156 kcals, protein 6g, carbs 14g, fat 9g, sat fat 1g, fibre 4g, sugar 2g, salt 0.82g

Parmesan-roasted potatoes

If you thought you couldn't improve on the classic roastie, try these – so good they could be a savoury snack in their own right.

TAKES 1 HOUR ● SERVES 6

1.8kg/4lb floury potatoes, cut in half, or quarters if large
5 tbsp olive oil
2 tsp plain flour
100g/4oz Parmesan, finely grated
handful of parsley leaves, finely chopped
4 rosemary sprigs, leaves finely chopped
pinch of grated nutmeg

1 Heat oven to 220C/200C fan/gas 7. Put the potatoes in a pan of salted water, bring to the boil, then simmer for 2 minutes. Drain, then toss in a little oil.
2 Stir together the flour, Parmesan, herbs and nutmeg with a small pinch of salt, then toss the potatoes in the mix until evenly coated.
3 Heat a good layer of oil in a shallow, non-stick roasting tin on the hob, then carefully add the potatoes. Turn the potatoes to coat them in the oil, then roast in the oven for 40 minutes, turning once, until crisp and browned.

PER SERVING 339 kcals, protein 11g, carbs 43g, fat 15g, sat fat 5g, fibre 3g, sugar 2g, salt 0.36g

Roast tomatoes with pesto

The shortest recipe in the book, and perhaps the sweetest. These tomatoes will go with just about anything and are so easy to prepare.

TAKES 25 MINUTES • SERVES 4–6, EASILY DOUBLED
6 large tomatoes
3 tbsp pesto

1 Heat oven to 190C/170C fan/gas 5. Halve the tomatoes and arrange them in a single layer, cut-side up, in a roasting tin. Spoon some pesto over each tomato, then roast for 20 minutes, until the tomatoes are tender.

PER SERVING 73 kcals, protein 4g, carbs 7g, fat 4g, sat fat 1g, fibre 2g, sugar 7g, salt 0.2g

White bean, parsley & garlic mash

Canned beans and chickpeas are perfect for mashing when you need a speedy side dish.

TAKES 15 MINUTES • SERVES 4

2 tbsp olive oil
2 shallots or ½ small onion, finely
   chopped
2 garlic cloves, chopped
2 × 400g cans cannellini beans,
   drained and rinsed
50ml/2fl oz chicken or vegetable stock,
   or use water
handful of flat-leaf parsley, leaves
   roughly chopped

1 Heat the oil in a pan and tip in the shallots or onion. Gently cook for 5 minutes, add the garlic, then give it another 2 minutes until soft.
2 Tip the beans into the pan and roughly mash. Add the stock or water to loosen the mixture, warm through, stir in the parsley, then season and serve.

PER SERVING 189 kcals, protein 10g, carbs 23g, fat 7g, sat fat 1g, fibre 7g, sugar 3g, salt 1.34g

Layered roast summer vegetables

This dish can double up as a veggie main course that is perfect for summer. It's incredibly good for you, too, with each portion including all of your 5-a-day!

TAKES 1½ HOURS • SERVES 4

6 tbsp good-quality olive oil
4 large courgettes, thickly sliced
   (yellow ones look pretty)
5 ripe plum tomatoes, sliced
2 aubergines, sliced
1 large garlic bulb, kept whole
small bunch of rosemary, broken into
   sprigs

1 Heat oven to 220C/200C fan/gas 7. Drizzle a little oil over the base of a round ovenproof dish. Starting from the outside, tightly layer alternate slices of the vegetables over the base in concentric circles until you get to the middle – sit the garlic here. If you have any vegetables left, tuck them into gaps around the outside.

2 Stick the sprigs of rosemary among the vegetables, drizzle everything generously with more oil, then season with salt and black pepper. Roast everything together, drizzling with more oil occasionally, for 50 minutes–1 hour until the vegetables are soft and lightly charred.

3 Remove from the oven and leave to stand for a few minutes, then remove the garlic and separate it into cloves for squeezing over the vegetables.

PER SERVING 240 kcals, protein 7g, carbs 12g, fat 18g, sat fat 3g, fibre 7g, sugar 11g, salt 0.54g

Creamy cheese & tomato macaroni

Despite its indulgent-sounding name, this simple side is good for you and low in fat. Try serving it with tomato-based stews and casseroles.

TAKES 20 MINUTES • SERVES 4

300g/10oz macaroni or other small pasta shapes
25g/1oz sun-dried tomatoes in oil, drained and roughly chopped
2 tbsp crème fraîche
1 tbsp tomato purée
1 tbsp grated Parmesan

1 Boil the pasta according to the packet instructions. Meanwhile, in a small food processor, blitz together the tomatoes, crème fraîche and tomato purée into a sauce. (If you don't have a small processor, finely chop the tomatoes, then mix everything together.)

2 Drain the pasta, saving a little of the cooking water, then return to the pan with the tomato sauce, the reserved cooking water and half the cheese. Mix together until all the pasta is coated, then serve sprinkled with the remaining cheese.

PER SERVING 314 kcals, protein 11g, carbs 58g, fat 6g, sat fat 3g, fibre 3g, sugar 3g, salt 0.33g

Broccoli with chilli & crispy garlic

Chilli and garlic really add a zing to your meal. Tenderstem can be substituted for ordinary broccoli, or try with green beans or kale instead, depending on the season.

TAKES 10 MINUTES ● **SERVES 6–8, EASILY HALVED**

400g/14oz Tenderstem broccoli, stalks and florets separated

3 garlic cloves, thinly sliced

4 tbsp olive oil

1 red chilli, deseeded and sliced

1 Bring a large pan of salted water to the boil, add the broccoli stalks and cook for 2 minutes, then add the florets and cook for 2 minutes more.

2 Gently heat the garlic and oil together until the garlic just starts to sizzle and brown, then remove from the heat and add the chilli. Drain the broccoli really well and toss in the garlic oil to serve.

PER SERVING 85 kcals, protein 2g, carbs 2g, fat 8g, sat fat 1g, fibre 2g, sugar 2g, salt 0.02g

Green beans with garlic & white wine vinegar

These beans are served at room temperature, having been marinated in vinegar.
They are really good with roast meat or a barbecue.

TAKES 10 MINUTES ● SERVES 4

200g pack green beans
2–3 tbsp white wine vinegar, to taste
3 tbsp extra-virgin olive oil
1 garlic clove, finely sliced

1 Boil the beans in plenty of salted water for 5–8 minutes until cooked through. Drain and, while still hot, toss with the vinegar, oil and garlic. Adjust the seasoning and vinegar to taste. Serve at room temperature.

PER SERVING 87 kcals, protein 1g, carbs 2g, fat 9g, sat fat 1g, fibre 1g, sugar 1g, salt none

Fennel gratin

Enjoy this with lamb, or even by itself with lots of crusty bread. For another easy side dish idea, swap the fennel for halved onions.

TAKES 30 MINUTES • SERVES 4

4 large fennel bulbs
pinch of grated nutmeg
1 garlic clove, crushed
200ml/7fl oz double cream
50g/2oz Parmesan, grated

1 Heat oven to 200C/180C fan/gas 6 and put a pan of salted water on to boil. Trim the fennel tops, then cut the fennel into wedges. Boil for 5 minutes, then drain well and put into a baking dish. Sprinkle with the nutmeg.

2 Stir the garlic into the cream and pour it over the fennel. Top with the Parmesan, then bake for 20 minutes until golden.

PER SERVING 320 kcals, protein 7g, carbs 4g, fat 31g, sat fat 17g, fibre 3g, sugar 3g, salt 0.56g

Best-ever tiramisu

Like a trifle, tiramisu benefits from being made ahead, giving time for all the lovely flavours to mingle.

TAKES 30 MINUTES, PLUS CHILLING
● **SERVES 6**

568ml pot double cream
250g tub mascarpone
75ml/2½fl oz Marsala
5 tbsp golden caster sugar
300ml/½ pint strong coffee, made with
    2 tbsp instant coffee granules mixed
    with 300ml/½ pint boiling water
175g pack sponge fingers
25g/1oz chunk dark chocolate
2 tsp cocoa powder, to dust

1 Put the cream, mascarpone, Marsala and sugar in a large bowl. Whisk until the cream and mascarpone have completely combined and have the consistency of thickly whipped cream.

2 Put the coffee into a shallow bowl and dip in a few sponge fingers at a time, turning for a few seconds until they are nicely soaked, but not soggy. Layer these into a serving dish until half the biscuits have been used, then spread over half of the cream mixture. Using the coarse side of a grater, grate over most of the chocolate. Then repeat the layers, using up all the coffee, and finish with a cream layer.

3 Cover and chill for a few hours or overnight. This can now be kept in the fridge for up to 2 days. To serve, dust with cocoa and grate over the remainder of the chocolate.

PER SERVING 853 kcals, protein 5g, carbs 44g, fat 73g, sat fat 42g, fibre 1g, sugar 35g, salt 0.25g

Balsamic blueberries with vanilla ice cream

Poaching blueberries really brings out their flavour, especially with a dash of balsamic vinegar. Serve warm or cold over good-quality ice cream.

TAKES 15 MINUTES • SERVES 2, EASILY DOUBLED

125g/4½oz blueberries
1 tbsp caster sugar
1 tsp balsamic vinegar
4 scoops good-quality vanilla ice cream
crisp biscuits, to serve

1 Tip the blueberries into a pan with the sugar, vinegar and 1 tablespoon water. Heat very gently for 1–2 minutes until the berries soften but don't burst. Set aside until ready to serve.

2 Serve spooned over the ice cream and eat with crisp biscuits.

PER SERVING (without biscuits) 262 kcals, protein 5g, carbs 36g, fat 12g, sat fat 8g, fibre 1g, sugar 35g, salt 0.19g

Pine nut & honey tart

If you haven't tried pine nuts in a sweet recipe before, give this a go. This is known as a crostata *in Italy, but it's best described here as a honeyed version of Bakewell tart.*

TAKES ABOUT 1½ HOURS, PLUS SOAKING AND CHILLING
- **SERVES 8–10**

100g/4oz raisins
140g/5oz mixed glacé fruit, chopped
3 tbsp rum or orange juice
300g/10oz sweet dessert pastry
50g/2oz plain flour, plus extra for dusting
175g/6oz softened butter
175g/6oz golden caster sugar
175g/6oz ground almonds
5 eggs, beaten
85g/3oz pine nuts
2 tbsp clear honey, plus extra for drizzling

1 Put the raisins and glacé fruit in a bowl with the rum or orange juice, then soak for 1 hour. Roll the pastry on a floured surface and use it to line a 23cm loose-bottomed tart tin. Leave the pastry overhanging the edges, prick the base, then chill for 1 hour.

2 Heat oven to 200C/180C fan/gas 6. Fill the pastry case with baking paper and baking beans, then blind-bake for 8 minutes. Remove the paper and beans, then bake for about 5 minutes more. Allow to cool a little.

3 Beat together the flour, butter, sugar, almonds and eggs. Stir in the fruit, then pour into the pastry case. Scatter over the pine nuts, press lightly into the surface, then drizzle over the honey.

4 Return the tart to the oven, lower the heat to 180C/160C fan/gas 4 and bake for 40–50 minutes until firm. If the top browns too quickly, cover with foil. Cool in the tin. Serve with the extra honey.

PER SERVING 665 kcals, protein 11g, carbs 61g, fat 43g, sat fat 15g, fibre 3g, sugar 45g, salt 0.56g

Double cherry semifreddo

You might have come across this style of ice cream in Italian restaurants. It's light and creamy and, best of all, you don't need an ice-cream maker to prepare it.

TAKES 35 MINUTES, PLUS FREEZING AND COOLING • SERVES 8

1kg/2lb 4oz cherries, stones removed
400ml/14fl oz double cream
100g/4oz icing sugar
4 eggs, separated
wafers, to serve (optional)

1 Set aside 50g/2oz cherries and put the rest in a pan with the cream and half the icing sugar. Bring to the boil, then gently simmer for 5 minutes. Whizz in a blender.

2 Pour a little of the hot cherry mix over the egg yolks, whisk well, then pour back into the pan. Cook for about 5 minutes more or until thickened a little and the mixture coats the back of a wooden spoon. Sieve into a bowl, cover the surface with cling film, then set aside to cool completely.

3 In another bowl, whisk the egg whites until stiff then whisk in the remaining sugar, 1 tablespoon at a time, until the mixture looks like shaving foam. Fold the mixture into the cherry cream in three batches.

4 Line a 900g loaf tin with cling film, fill with the mix then freeze for 3 hours. Remove from the freezer, stir in the reserved cherries, then freeze overnight.

PER SERVING 400 kcals, protein 5g, carbs 29g, fat 30g, sat fat 16g, fibre none, sugar 28g, salt 0.15g

Spiced arancello

Boozy, spiced and sweet, this liqueur is based on the classic Italian drink Arancello. It is superb served straight, over ice, or it will give an exquisite orangey kick to ice cream.

TAKES 1¼ HOURS, PLUS 2 WEEKS STANDING • MAKES ABOUT 2.5 LITRES

5 large oranges
1 cinnamon stick
2–3 cardamom pods
1 vanilla pod
1-litre bottle vodka
600g/1lb 5oz caster sugar
a few extra oranges, cinnamon sticks, cardamom and vanilla pods, to decorate

1 Pare the zest from the oranges using a peeler, making sure that none of the bitter white pith is left on the peel. Put the zest, spices and vanilla pod in one large or several smaller clean jars, then tip in the vodka. Seal and leave for a week, shaking the jar or jars every day.
2 After a week you're ready for the next stage. Boil a kettle of water. Put the sugar in a heatproof bowl, then pour over 500ml/16fl oz boiling water, stirring until the sugar dissolves. Add this to the vodka mix, then leave for another week, shaking the jar or jars regularly.
3 Strain into bottles, discarding the peel and spices, and store in a cool place. If you are giving bottles as a gift, drop some fresh spices and peel into each bottle to decorate. Will keep bottled for 6 months.

PER SERVING (85ml) 179 kcals, protein none, carbs 27g, fat none, sat fat none, fibre none, sugar 27g, salt none

Raspberry mascarpone trifle

Mascarpone adds lightness and a creamy note to this speedy trifle. You could add a dash of Amaretto to the sponge instead of the cassis, if you prefer.

TAKES 20 MINUTES ● **SERVES 6**

10–12 sponge fingers
400g/14oz fresh or frozen raspberries
juice of 2 oranges
1 tbsp cassis
250g tub mascarpone
500ml pot fresh vanilla custard

1 Break the sponge fingers into a large bowl then scatter over 300g/10oz of the raspberries, the orange juice and the cassis. Leave to soak for 15 minutes.
2 Beat the mascarpone in a large bowl until smooth then beat in the custard. Spoon over the sponge, scatter over the remaining raspberries, then serve.

PER SERVING 343 kcals, protein 5g, carbs 27g, fat 25g, sat fat 15g, fibre 2g, sugar 21g, salt 0.24g

White chocolate creams with balsamic strawberries

Chill this for at least an hour before serving as the flavours seem to get even better. If you're worried about the raw egg, just leave it out.

TAKES 20 MINUTES, PLUS CHILLING
- **SERVES 2**

100g/4oz white chocolate, broken into small pieces

2 small handfuls of strawberries, roughly chopped, plus 1 extra strawberry, halved, to decorate

1 tbsp balsamic vinegar

1 tsp clear honey

142ml pot double cream

1 egg yolk

2 shortbread biscuits, crumbled, to decorate

1 Melt the chocolate in a bowl set over a pan of hot, but not boiling, water, making sure the bowl does not touch the water. Allow to cool slightly.

2 Meanwhile, mix together the chopped strawberries, vinegar and honey. Spoon the strawberries into two glasses or bowls, leaving behind any excess vinegar. Whip the cream until thick.

3 Stir the egg yolk into the cooled melted chocolate (if it stiffens up too much, stir in 1 tablespoon hot water to loosen it a little). Using electric beaters, briefly whisk in a third of the whipped cream until the chocolate mixture is smooth. Fold in the remaining cream with a spatula or metal spoon, divide between the glasses over the strawberries and chill for at least half an hour, if you have time.

4 To serve, sprinkle the creams with the crumbled shortbread and top each with a strawberry half.

PER SERVING 764 kcals, protein 8g, carbs 45g, fat 63g, sat fat 35g, fibre 1g, sugar 38g, salt 0.3g

Citrus grape cake

This lovely rustic cake is based on a bake from Tuscany, and we've used olive oil and butter to maintain that Mediterranean feel. Try it warm or cold.

TAKES 1 HOUR 5 MINUTES, PLUS COOLING • SERVES 8–10

225ml/8fl oz dessert wine (muscat will give the best result)

175ml/6fl oz extra-virgin olive oil, plus extra for greasing

225g/8½oz plain flour, plus 1 tbsp for dusting

200g/8oz light muscovado sugar

zest of 1 orange and 1 lemon

100g/4oz softened butter

3 large eggs

1 tsp baking powder

175g/6oz grapes, halved and seeded

4–5 tbsp demerara sugar

1 Reduce the wine in a pan until you have about 85ml/3fl oz – this will take 5–10 minutes. Cool.

2 Heat oven to 180C/160C fan/gas 4. Brush a 23cm springform cake tin with oil, tip in the 1 tablespoon flour, then shake all over the pan until covered. Discard any excess flour. Beat together the muscovado sugar, zests and butter until creamy then add the eggs, one at a time.

3 Stir together the cooled wine and oil, then pour a little into the cake mix. Stir, then fold in a third of the flour and all the baking powder. Repeat twice more to make a smooth batter.

4 Spoon into the prepared tin, scatter the halved grapes over the top, then sprinkle with the demerara sugar. Bake for around 35–40 minutes until a skewer inserted into the middle of the cake comes out clean.

PER SERVING 574 kcals, protein 6g, carbs 62g, fat 33g, sat fat 10g, fibre 1g, sugar 39g, salt 0.49g

Iced hazelnut zabagliones

This recipe makes more than you'll need for two, but once you've tried these little puds, you'll be glad there's more in the freezer.

TAKES 30 MINUTES, PLUS FREEZING
● **SERVES 2 (OR UP TO 6)**

100g pack hazelnuts, toasted and very
  roughly chopped
400ml/14fl oz double cream
85g/3oz golden caster sugar, plus
  1 tbsp
3 egg yolks
5 tbsp sweet Marsala
FOR THE COFFEE MARSALA SAUCE
4 tbsp chocolate hazelnut spread
2 tbsp sweet Marsala
2 tsp instant coffee, dissolved in 2 tbsp
  boiling water

1 Whizz all but 1 tablespoon of the nuts in a food processor until fine. Whip the cream with 1 tablespoon sugar. Dissolve the remaining sugar in 100ml/3½fl oz water, then boil for 1 minute.

2 Line two individual basins with cling film, leaving enough overhang to cover. Put the egg yolks and Marsala into a large bowl set over a pan of hot water and whisk until foamy. Trickle in the sugar syrup with the beaters running. Keep beating for about 5 minutes until the mixture is thick and holds a trail. Take off the heat then whisk until cooled. Whisk in the cream, then fold in the ground nuts.

3 Spoon into the moulds, then fold the cling film over the top (put the leftover mixture in a tub). Freeze overnight.

4 On the day of serving, put all the sauce ingredients into a small pan, whisk till boiling, then cool. Serve the zabagliones with the sauce and chopped nuts.

PER SERVING 621 kcals, protein 6g, carbs 27g, fat 53g, sat fat 22g, fibre 1g, sugar 27g, salt 0.07g

Bicerin

Bicerin is a luxurious coffee-and-chocolate drink topped with cream that originates from a café in Turin, where the recipe is a closely guarded secret. Here is our version.

TAKES 10 MINUTES ● SERVES 2

200ml/7fl oz whole milk

2 heaped tbsp good-quality drinking chocolate or finely chopped dark chocolate

4 tbsp single or double cream

150ml/¼ pint espresso or very strong, hot coffee

sugar, to taste

1 Heat the milk in a small pan. When the milk is just boiling, whisk in the drinking chocolate or chocolate until smooth.

2 Whisk the cream until frothy. Pour the coffee into two heatproof glasses, then add sugar to taste. Pour in the hot chocolate. Top with the cream, then enjoy straight away.

PER SERVING 211 kcals, protein 5g, carbs 25g, fat 11g, sat fat 7g, fibre none, sugar 24g, salt 0.24g

Melon granita

The nice thing about making a granita is that you don't need a machine – an ice-cream maker would in fact make it too smooth and turn it into a sorbet.

TAKES 35–45 MINUTES, PLUS FREEZING • SERVES 8 GENEROUSLY

100g/4oz caster sugar
1 vanilla pod, split lengthways
2 very ripe charentais (orange-fleshed) melons, cut in half and deseeded
juice of ½ lemon

1 Tip the sugar and 125ml/4fl oz water into a pan. Scrape in the vanilla seeds and put in the pod as well, then heat gently until the sugar has dissolved. Bring to the boil and boil for 6–8 minutes to make a sugar syrup. Leave to cool then remove the vanilla pod.

2 Scoop the melon flesh on to a board and chop to a slush with a sharp knife (or you can do this in a food processor). Mix the sugar syrup, slush and lemon juice in a large, shallow baking dish.

3 Freeze, uncovered, in the dish for about 1 hour until crystals form around the edges. With a fork, stir the edges into the centre and mash well, then freeze until crystals form again. Stir and refreeze every half an hour or so until the granita is frozen all over – this should take about 3 hours. Fork it up roughly to serve. For the best flavour, enjoy within 1 week.

PER SERVING 69 kcals, protein 1g, carbs 18g, fat none, sat fat none, fibre 1g, added sugar 13g, salt 0.02g

Orange frosted panettone cake

Topped and filled with mascarpone frosting, an Italian panettone makes a wonderfully quick, but impressive alternative Christmas cake.

TAKES ABOUT 15 MINUTES • SERVES 8

500g boxed fruity panettone (or pick a chocolate one if you don't like dried fruit)

500g tub mascarpone

zest 1 orange

2 tbsp caster sugar

silver balls, to decorate (optional)

FOR THE SYRUP

juice 2 oranges, zest of 1

2 tbsp caster sugar

1 tbsp Grand Marnier

1 Make the syrup first. Gently heat all the ingredients together until the sugar dissolves, then boil for 1 minute or until just thickened. Leave to cool.

2 Meanwhile, trim the rounded top off the panettone (this is cook's perks for later!), then cut the rest into 4 horizontal slices using a serrated knife. Beat the mascarpone, orange zest and caster sugar together.

3 Stack up the slices, drizzling a little of the orange syrup over each piece as you go, and using about 2 tablespoons of the mascarpone to sandwich each layer together. Once you've finished stacking, cover with the rest of the mascarpone in swirls and whirls – a palette knife is the best tool for the job. Scatter with a few silver balls if you like, then serve straight away, or chill for up to 2 hours, then scatter with the balls at the last minute.

PER SERVING 560 kcals, protein 6g, carbs 48g, fat 39g, sat fat 22g, fibre 1g, sugar 34g, salt 0.48g

Amaretti mocha roulade

Aside from being filled with delicious Italian flavours, the biggest selling point for this roulade is that it can be made the day before eating, then left in the fridge until needed.

TAKES ABOUT 1 HOUR, PLUS COOLING

- **SERVES 6**

2 × 100g bars dark chocolate flavoured with coffee, broken into squares, of which 25g/1oz finely chopped

6 eggs, separated

175g/6oz dark brown soft sugar, plus extra 1 tbsp

2 tbsp cocoa powder

85g/3oz amaretti biscuits, finely crushed

284ml pot double cream

3 tbsp Tia Maria, plus extra to drizzle (optional)

1 Heat oven to 180C/160C fan/gas 4. Line a greased 23x33cm Swiss-roll tin with baking parchment. Melt the 175g/6oz chocolate squares in a bowl set over a pan of just simmering water.

2 In a bowl, whisk together the egg yolks and sugar until thick and creamy. With clean whisks and in a separate bowl, whisk the egg whites until stiff. Fold the melted chocolate into the yolk mixture, then fold in the whites, then the cocoa. Pour into the tin; bake for 18 minutes.

3 Put a sheet of baking parchment on a tea towel and sprinkle with the crushed biscuits. Turn out the roulade on to the paper, then peel away the lining paper. Trim the edges, then roll up the sponge.

4 Whip the cream with the 1 tablespoon of sugar and the Tia Maria until stiff. Carefully unroll the cooled roulade, fill it with cream and the finely chopped chocolate, then roll it up. Serve drizzled with a little more Tia Maria, if you like.

PER SERVING 710 kcals, protein 11g, carbs 71g, fat 44g, sat fat 22g, fibre 1g, sugar 62g, salt 0.41g

Index